MONITORS OF THE ROYAL NAVY

MONITORS OF THE ROYAL NAVY

HOW THE FLEET BROUGHT THE GREAT GUNS TO BEAR

The Story of the Monitors in Two World Wars

BY

JIM CROSSLEY

Pen & Sword
MARITIME

First published in Great Britain in 2013 and reprinted in this format by
Pen & Sword Maritime
an imprint of
Pen & Sword Books Ltd
47 Church Street
Barnsley
South Yorkshire
S70 2AS

ISBN 978 1 47387 714 6

A CIP catalogue record for this book is
available from the British Library.

Typeset in Palatino by
Phoenix Typesetting, Auldgirth, Dumfriesshire

Printed and bound in England by
CPI Group (UK) Ltd, Croydon, CR0 4YY

Pen & Sword Books Ltd incorporates the Imprints of Pen & Sword
Aviation, Pen & Sword Family History, Pen & Sword Maritime,
Pen & Sword Military, Pen & Sword Discovery, Pen and Sword Fiction,
Pen and Sword History, Wharncliffe Local History, Wharncliffe True
Crime, Wharncliffe Transport, Pen & Sword Select, Pen & Sword
Military Classics, Leo Cooper, The Praetorian Press, Seaforth Publishing
and Frontline Publishing

For a complete list of Pen & Sword titles please contact
PEN & SWORD BOOKS LIMITED
47 Church Street, Barnsley, South Yorkshire, S70 2AS, England
E-mail: enquiries@pen-and-sword.co.uk
Website: www.pen-and-sword.co.uk

Contents

List of Maps

Acknowledgements

Ian Buxton's book *Big Gun Monitors* gives an excellent detailed account of the construction and deployment of the monitors, and particularly of their main armament.

Severn's Saga by E. Keble Chatterton is a most interesting account of operations in East Africa.

The Dover Patrol (Two Volumes) by Sir Reginald Bacon, *The Keyes Papers* (Two Volumes), and Roger Keyes's *Naval Memoirs* give a good insight into the bombardment of the Belgian Coast. Keyes also gives an interesting if rather one sided account of the Dardanelles campaign.

Castles of Steel by Robert Massie is an excellent general account of naval affairs during the First World War and *Engage the Enemy More Closely* by Correlli Barnet is an excellent history of the Royal Navy in the Second World War.

D-Day by Anthony Beevor is a first class account of the Normandy landings.

Walcheren 1944 by Richard Brooks is an excellent source of information on this action.

Battleship by H.P. Wilmott is an excellent exposition of the evolution and use of battleships.

There are many other useful source books including Corbett, Madden and Jellicoe on the First World War and Roskill on the Second World War.

Photographs by permission of the Imperial War Museum.

Map 1

The Belgian
Coast Showing
Gun Positions
Existing in 1918

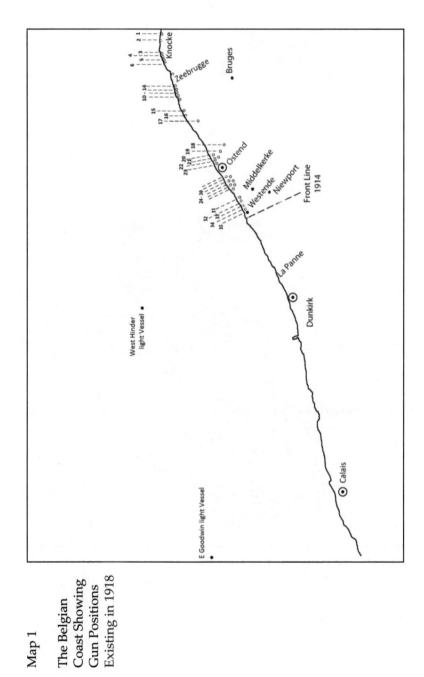

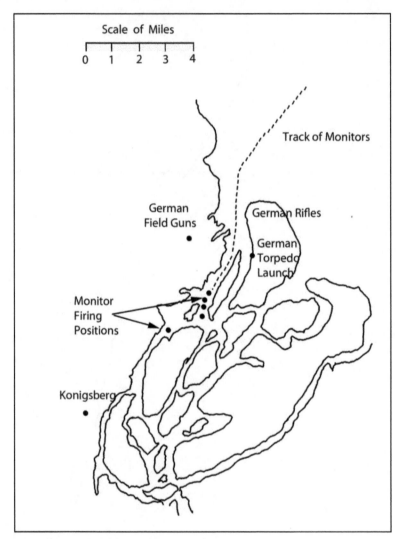

Map 2 - The Rufiji Delta

Map 3 -
The
Dardanelles

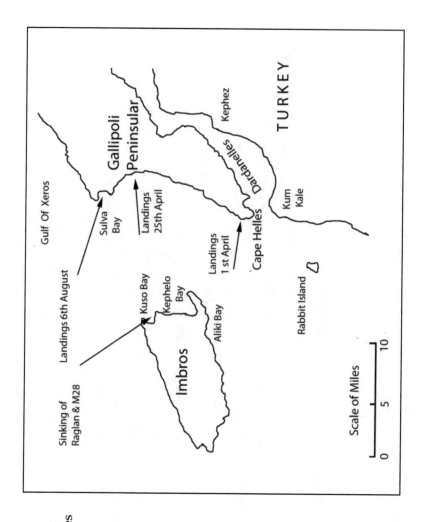

Gulf Of Xeros

Sinking of
Raglan & M28

Landings 6th August

Sulva
Bay

Gallipoli
Peninsular

Landings
25th April

Kuso Bay

Kephelo
Bay

Imbros

Aliki Bay

Landings
1 st April

Cape Helles

Dardanelles

Kephez

Kum
Kale

TURKEY

Rabbit Island

Scale of Miles

0   5   10

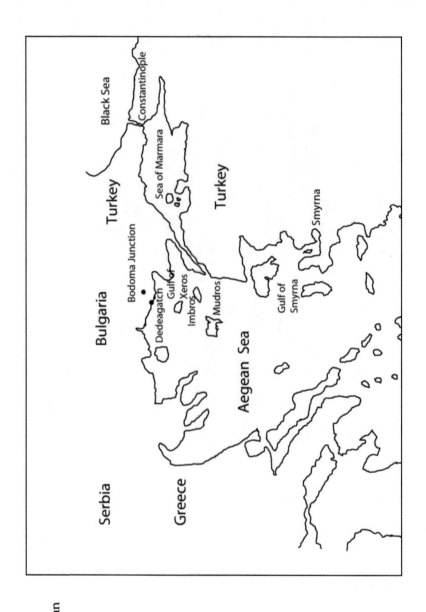

Map 4 -
The Aegean

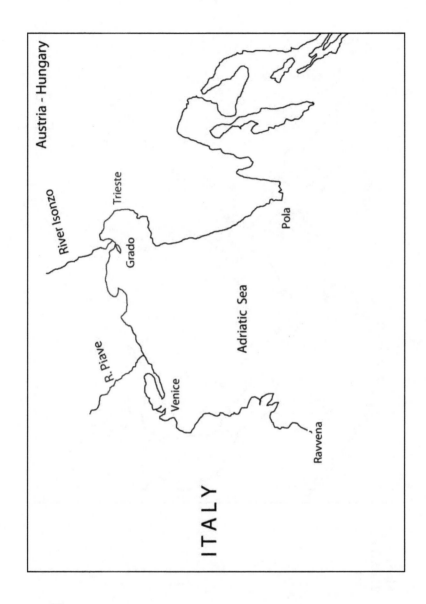

Map 5 -
The Gulf of
Trieste

Austria - Hungary

River Isonzo

Trieste

Grado

Pola

Adriatic Sea

R. Piave

Venice

Ravvena

ITALY

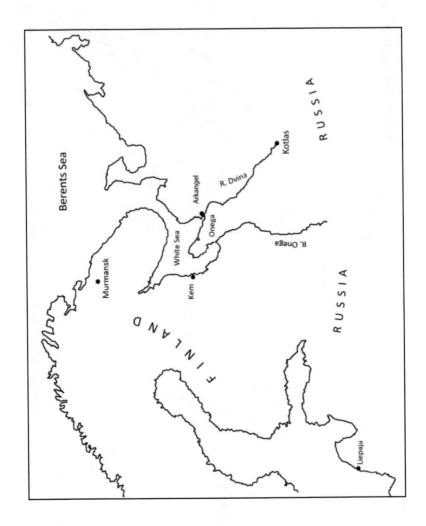

Map 6 -
The White
Sea

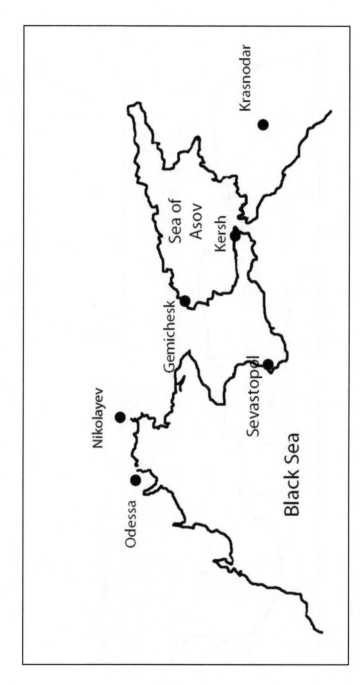

Map 7 - The Sea of Azov

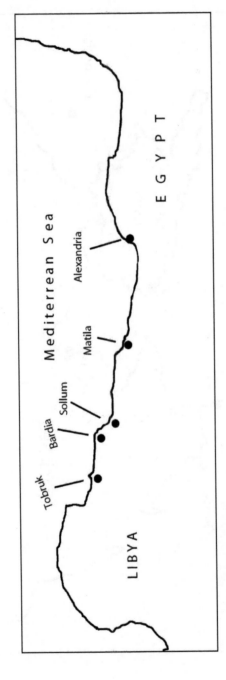

Map 8 - North African Coast

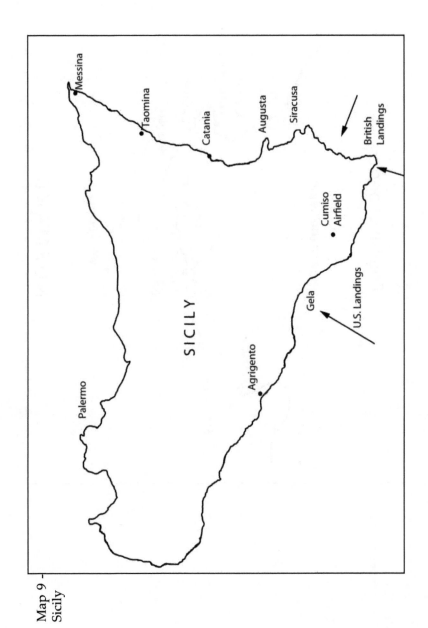

Map 9
Sicily

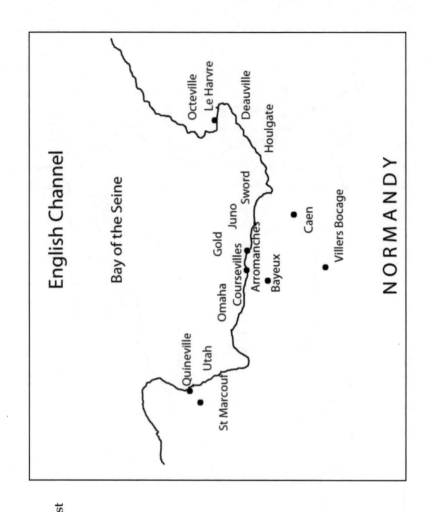

Map 10 -
The Normandy Coast

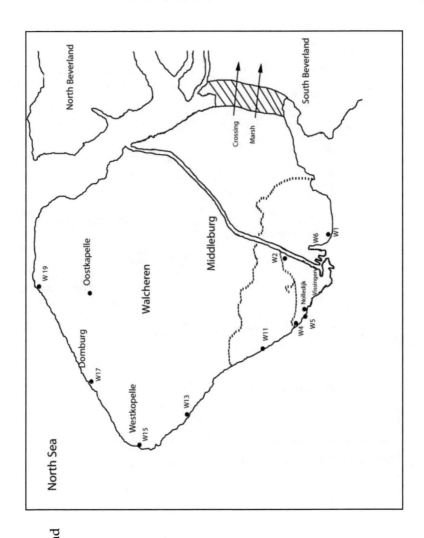

Map 11 -
Walcheren Island

Map 12 - The Gulf of Salerno

Chapter 1

Origins

In the 1690s an entirely new class of warship caused consternation and a crisis of conscience to the English ruling classes. The offender was the "bomb ketch", a vessel copied from the French. Bomb ketches were small, shallow draft ships, able to get close inshore. They were armed with a dastardly weapon, a large bore mortar, which threw an explosive bomb far up in the air so that it cleared the walls of waterside cities or harbours and exploded when it struck the ground, damaging property and killing soldiers and civilians alike. The British used them thus to bombard St Malo, Le Havre, Dieppe and Dunkirk. John Evelyn, the diarist, wrote that the Navy should be employed to protect British shipping not "Spending their time bombing and ruining a few paltry little towns . . . a hostility totally averse to humanity and especially to Christianity", however the bomb vessels, Christian or otherwise, continued to be developed and used. They fought the French off Gibraltar, where in a flat calm they engaged and severely damaged some French ships of the line, and at Toulon, where the fire from English and Dutch "bombs" destroyed several ships in harbour and caused the French to panic and scuttle the remains of their battle fleet at its moorings. This was a particularly significant action in that the Allies had landed observers ashore to watch the fall of shot and signal corrections to the gun layers afloat. This practice became frequently used when bomb vessels were employed, and a special force of observers were trained and retained by the Ordinance Board to undertake these duties. They would go to sea in tenders, one of which was attached to each bomb vessel, to accommodate them and to carry spare ammunition.

These useful vessels remained in service throughout the eighteenth and the first part of the nineteenth centuries. A typical action was at Copenhagen in 1807. Britain was attempting to prevent the Danish fleet falling into French hands, following the agreement between Napoleon and the Tsar at Tilsit. The Danes refused to hand their ships to Britain "for safe keeping" and a fleet under Admiral Gambier accompanied by a force of 25,000 soldiers set out to compel them to do so. *Thunder, Vesuvius, Aetna* and *Zebra*, all bomb ketches, bombarded the fortress of Trekroner, in the approaches to Copenhagen, while troops and artillery advanced on land. After a pause for negotiation, which proved fruitless, fire was opened on the city itself as well as the fortress. This time, the efforts of the bomb vessels were supported by land based cannon and mortars. A huge timber yard was set on fire and eventually the city itself was in flames. The Danes capitulated and their fleet was captured or destroyed. In subsequent skirmishing *Thunder* was in action against Danish oared gun boats which she success-fully drove off by using her mortar to fire "air bursting" bombs which exploded over their target, showering it with lead balls.

During the Crimean War (1854-6) both French and British

navies employed a number of bomb vessels and also developed a class of barges fitted with heavy mortars to engage targets on land. The first of these barges built in Britain had names, but subsequently they were only given numbers, a practice to be continued for the small monitors built many years later.

The bomb vessels of the nineteenth century shared many characteristics with their early forebears and indeed with the bombardment vessels of the two twentieth century world wars. Their primary role was shore bombardment and to achieve this they needed very heavy weapons which could out range or out shoot shore based artillery. Most of these ships had two mortars, one 13 inch and one 10 inch. To support the recoil of these enormous weapons vessels had to be extremely heavily built, and to fire at all accurately they had to be very stable. This, together with the need for shallow draft, so as to get close to the enemy fortifications, resulted in ships with a very broad beam and poor sailing qualities. Their appetite for heavy ammunition meant that they required capacious tenders. Early ships had indeed been "bomb ketches" – ketch rigged vessels with a fore and aft mainsail on a mast set well back in the hull – the mortar fired forwards, over the bows. They must have been horrors to handle. Later "bombs" were "ship rigged" with three masts, but they remained slow and unhandy at sea. When the ships were not required for their main purpose the mortars would be removed and replaced with conventional armament so that they could be rated as sloops and undertake convoy duties, although in this role they must sometimes have had problems keeping up with their charges. Conversely in war time merchant vessels were often requisitioned and converted into makeshift "bombs". A very suitable occupation for naval bomb vessels in peace time was polar exploration, for which their very strong build and shallow draft made them ideal. *Erebus* and *Terror* – names which we will encounter again later – made an epic voyage to the Antarctic in 1841 and 1842 which included being severely damaged by ice, battered by gales, threatened by enormous ice-bergs and finally a near fatal collision. No ships except bomb vessels would have survived such hazards.

The adventures of these wooden sailing vessels may seem far removed from those of the monitors of the twentieth century, but in fact they are closely related. Both were small shallow draft ships, slow and unhandy but mounting massive fire power. Both were unsuitable for fighting other ships at sea but could be devastatingly effective against targets on land or enemy ships in harbour. Above all they both needed to work in close co-operation with land forces. This involved communicating effectively with observers on land (or later in the air), understanding the military situation and bringing down their massive fire power on the right spot at the right moment. At the same time they had to be relatively cheap ships with small crews, since they would be required to operate at great risk to themselves close under the guns of enemy fortifications, where it would be foolish to hazard a valuable ship of the line

Experience gained over many years of operating these vessels was absorbed somewhere in the memory of the Admiralty and brought once again into the light of day in 1914.

A more direct ancestor of the twentieth century monitors was the USS *Monitor* herself. During the American civil war control of the river systems of the United States was critical to the whole logistical system of both armies. In the struggle to gain control of these the Federal navy evolved a type of ship which gave its name to the monitors of the future and displayed some of their salient characteristics.

Early in the civil war the Confederates had captured the US Navy yard at Norfolk, Virginia and so gained control of the access to the James River and the Elizabeth River. The mouth of the river system at Hampton Roads however was closely blockaded by the powerful Federal navy. The blockading squadron consisted of conventional sailing frigates, mostly with auxiliary steam engines, and supporting vessels including gun boats and armed tugs.

Determined to break the blockade, the Confederates raised the auxiliary steam powered frigate USS *Merrimac* which had been sunk by the retreating Federal forces. Stephen Mallory, the Confederate Navy Secretary, insisted that she should be re-built not as a frigate, but as an armoured steamship which could break the Federal blockade once and for all. The vessel which emerged was by any standards a monstrosity. The masts and sails were gone and in their place the only parts of the ship above water consisted of an armoured deck house pierced by holes through which protruded her smooth bore cannon. The Confederates had no way of making or obtaining armour plate so they used railway irons rolled together in strips to achieve heavy but effective armoured protection. The funnel stuck up through the deck house and the engine and boilers were below the water line. On the bow there was an enormous iron ram. A small armoured conning tower was used as a captain's bridge. *Virginia,* as she was re-christened, was totally unseaworthy and extremely slow, with a maximum speed of about 5 knots. Due to the great weight of ironwork in her superstructure she drew 22 feet of water. It was reported that with full rudder and full engine power it took her thirty minutes to turn round.

Virginia, however, was no stranger than the ship which was to be her opponent. *Monitor* was the brainchild of a Swedish engineer John Ericsson. The rapidly developing engineering industry in the Federal states made her construction possible and she was built in a yard in New York harbour in record time. To modern eyes she was more like a surfaced submarine than a ship. The iron hull was almost entirely submerged, the only features showing above water being a small conning tower or "pilot house", a spindly funnel and a massive rotating gun turret carrying two 11 inch guns. Like her opponent she was very slow and incapable of making a sea voyage under her own power, but she drew only 10 feet and was reasonably manoeuvrable in still water. She had very nearly foundered on the way to Hampton Roads under tow, when big seas threatened to swamp her completely, water gushing in through every vent and opening in the hull. With her big guns, shallow draft and low speed, she actually anticipated the monitors of the twentieth century although her primary role was to sink enemy ships, not shore bombardment.

Virginia steamed downriver to face the Federal blockaders on the day before *Monitor* was ready for action. Her armoured sides proved impervious to the fire of the conventional warships in the roads; her own fire, delivered at close range from her 60 pounder main armament, was devastating. *Congress* was forced to surrender and set on fire and *Cumberland* was disabled then rammed and sunk. *Minnesota* was badly damaged and ran aground. By the time the cumbersome monster had finished with these three opponents evening was drawing on. Her day's work done,

Virginia retreated into the shelter of the Confederate shore batteries and waited to finish off the rest of the blockading squadron when daylight returned. Dawn however, brought with it a nasty surprise. Lurking behind the damaged *Minnesota* was *Monitor*, freshly arrived from her hazardous tow from her builders in New York and looking in the words of a witness "Like a plank afloat with a can on top of it." *Monitor* allowed her opponent to steam close to her, disregarding her gunfire as she approached, then opened up with her own 11 inch armament at close range. The age of the armour piercing high velocity shell had not arrived however and her massive missiles only dented improvised defences of her opponent. Disregarding *Monitor*'s fire *Virginia* made an unsuccessful attempt to finish off *Minnesota*, which only resulted her running herself aground, she then turned her attention to *Monitor* and tried to repeat the ramming manoeuvre with which she had done for *Cumberland* on the previous day. *Monitor* proved too agile for her however and was only struck a glancing blow which did little damage. Later, a hit from heavy missile on the conning tower injured *Monitor*'s captain but still did no serious damage to the ship. Eventually both contestants gave up the fight and withdrew. No one in the armoured ships on either side had been killed and only a few wounded. The river remained blockaded.

Neither ship outlasted this famous encounter for long. *Virginia* fell into Federal hands when their armies advanced and she was destroyed in harbour. *Monitor* sunk with loss of life while under tow in heavy weather off Cape Hatteras.

The inconclusive end of the Battle of Hampton Roads did not deter the Confederates from building further monitors. As the Civil War went on they commissioned several more boats resembling *Monitor* and also developed smaller river monitors and mortar firing barges for riverine bombardment. Modest in size, and able to undertake only a very limited number of roles, these little vessels were nevertheless the forerunners of a total revolution in warship design. Gone were the lofty masts and sails. Gone were the rows of broadside guns. Less than fifty years after Hampton Roads great dreadnought battleships would rule the seas. Their frowning gun turrets and armoured steel hulls descended directly from that "Plank with a tin can on it" which so astonished the world in March 1862.

The US Navy persisted with the development of monitors of various types until the turn of the nineteenth century, and Britain made some tentative experiments with similar types of vessel, but gradually the concept was allowed to fade away until the events of 1914 brought an the idea of the monitor as a coastal bombardment vessel sharply back into focus.

When Britain and her Allies went to war with the German Empire in August 1914, the Royal Navy was far bigger and more powerful than any other in the world, indeed the "two power standard", dear to the hearts of naval planners, insisted that it should exceed the might of any other two naval powers combined. As soon as the war broke out the public expected that a second Trafalgar would somehow be arranged which would justify the massive investment made in the Senior Service. The navy should steam to Kiel and defy the Germans to come out. They should mount a close blockade of the German coast, as once they had the French. They should land marines on the north German coast. They should at least do something. In fact they did do something and that was to retreat from the fleet anchorage at Scapa Flow to safer havens on the west coast of Scotland and in Northern Ireland until effective anti-submarine defences could be provided at Scapa. This hardly seemed Nelsonian but it was good strategy and good sense. In Nelson's day there were no mines or torpedoes, weapons which could enable a small craft, a submarine or a minelayer, to disable the most powerful of warships. A grand gesture of defiance on the enemy coast would probably have led to the destruction of a large part of the British fleet and the once-and-for-all loss of naval supremacy. Admiral, Sir John Jellicoe, the commander of the Grand Fleet, as Britain's powerful home fleet was called, understood this very well. He was, as Churchill once said, the one man who "could lose the war in an afternoon" by risking his ships where they might be ensnared by a mine-field or tricked into running over a submarine trap. He consequently played a very cautious game.

The Royal Navy did in fact blockade Germany, but in a novel and different way. Dominating the approaches to the Channel, the North Sea and the Baltic, Britain was able to use small warships and armed merchant cruisers to stop and search ships of all nations approaching northern Europe and prevent goods consigned to Germany from reaching their destination. This caused difficulties with neutral countries, especially the Scandinavians and the Dutch, but it grew grad-ually more effective and was eventually to result in famine and the collapse of industrial production in Germany. Everywhere the German merchant marine was quickly driven off the seas. This arduous and unrelenting patrol work actually held the key to the eventual downfall of the German war machine. It did not, however, do anything to impair the effectiveness of their armies in the first years of the war, or to impede their rapid advance through Belgium and deep into France, until the Allies halted their progress on the Marne and the land war in the west became a bloody, static slogging match.

With Churchill as First Lord of the Admiralty, the Royal Navy was not content to become a passive spectator of the great events taking place on the near continent. As the Germans stormed through Belgium he insisted on landing a force of Royal Marines to attempt to defend the port of Antwerp, indeed he actually accompanied the expedition himself. It was not a success. He also became excited about the possibility of deploying a naval brigade on the western front equipped with armoured cars, and had his staff dashing about buying up all the Rolls Royce chassis they could get to convert for the purpose. Even this was not enough to satisfy his restless determination that the navy should deliver a devastating blow at the enemy, and a number of aggressive schemes were suggested.

One such scheme was to help the Russians by attacking the German flank by means of a landing in Pomerania. A strike there, it was claimed, would be only 60 miles from Berlin and would be a deadly blow at the heart of the German Empire, linking up with the Russian Army advancing from the east. The force would be transported by the navy, using obsolescent pre-dreadnought battleships to provide covering heavy weapon support. It was certainly a bold strategy, but close examination revealed insuperable problems. The area was heavily defended with minefields and coastal artillery. The sea was too shallow for battleships to manoeuvre. The passage through the Kattegatt would give the enemy ample time to prepare to meet the challenge. Even if the force did manage to land, the problems of re-supply and reinforcement would be insuperable. In spite of all objections both Churchill and the veteran Admiral Jacky Fisher, who was summoned out of retirement to become First Sea Lord in November 1914, wished to push plans forward but the army took a more realistic attitude and the project was abandoned.

Another scheme was to seize the island of Borkum, which is situated at the mouth of the River Ems and is the western-most of the German East Frisian Islands. A British naval presence there would threaten the base of the German High Seas Fleet at Wilhelmshaven and would be a jumping off point for attacks on the whole German North Sea coast. Objections to this plan were similar to those of the Baltic enterprise. It would be immensely risky and held out the prospect of the elderly battleships being overwhelmed and having to be rescued by the Grand Fleet, thus giving the Germans the possibility of setting exactly the sort of trap of mines and torpedoes which Jellicoe so rightly feared.

The third scheme was closer to the heart of the majority in the Royal Navy as it was supposed to offer an easy victory achieved by naval and Royal Marine units only and because it presented a chance to avenge a disgraceful chapter in the history of the Senior Service.

In August 1914, just before war was declared, the German battle cruiser *Goeben* and the light cruiser *Breslau* were the only German warships in the Mediterranean theatre. They had been sent there to show off German military might, to threaten British communications with her empire, and to deny France the opportunity of shipping troops from her North African colonies to mainland Europe. None of these objectives could be achieved however if Italy joined the war on the side of the Allies, as the British and French Mediterranean fleets far outnumbered and out gunned the two Germans, and the Austrian battle fleet, which might have assisted *Goeben* in her mission, was bottled up in the northern part of the Adriatic. In these circumstances the German Commander, Admiral Souchon, decided to try to break out into the Atlantic where his two powerful ships could menace British merchant shipping. Commandeering coal from a German liner he steamed at high speed for Gibraltar, making a token attack on the Algerian port of Phillipville on the way. Urgent orders received from Berlin, however forced him to change his plans.

Turkey was dithering as to whether to make an alliance with the Central Powers, and the German government became convinced that the appearance of two modern warships off the Golden Horn would tip the scales in their favour. Souchon was thus ordered to turn round and make for Constantinople. Although war between Britain and Germany had not yet been declared the British Mediterranean Fleet had been ordered to shadow *Goeben* and two battle cruisers, *Indomitable* and *Indefatigable,* soon had her in sight, but she was a faster ship and outran them, then slipped into the port of Messina for more coal which she seized from another German merchant ship. As she was coaling it was announced that Britain was at war with Germany and Italy put out a statement asserting her neutrality.

The British were convinced that, now that war had been declared, *Goeben* and her consort would try to break out westward again towards Gibraltar and stationed their battle cruisers west of Sicily to intercept them. The light cruiser *Gloucester*, however, on watch off the Italian coast, observed the two ships leaving Messina and heading east. She took up a shadowing station. *Gloucester* was much faster than *Goeben* but she was only lightly armed. At first the Germans made a feint towards the Adriatic, but eventually they altered course to pass Cape Matapan and it was obvious that they were making for the Dardanelles. *Gloucester* reported accordingly. Unknown to Souchon four British armoured cruisers and eight destroyers under Admiral Troubridge, a descendant of one of Nelson's bravest captains, were cruising at the entrance to the Adriatic in a position to intercept him. The armoured cruisers were not individually a match for *Goeben* on a one to one basis, they were slow and mounted 9.5 inch guns against the German's 11 inch, but the four of them plus the *Gloucester* should have been more than capable of handling the two Germans. As they steamed to intercept however Troubridge began to have second thoughts. His chief, Admiral Sir Archibald Berkeley Milne, known to all his friends as "Arky-Barky", had shown him a signal from Churchill, as ever interfering in operational affairs which should have been left to the First Sea Lord, telling him to refrain from engaging superior enemy forces. Churchill was intending to refer to the Austrian dreadnoughts lurking in the Adriatic, not to *Goeben*, but that was not what his signal said. Typical products of the early twentieth century navy, Arky-Barky and Troubridge were conditioned not to think for themselves but to obey orders to the letter. Troubridge's flag captain pointed out that with her superior speed and 11 inch guns, *Goeben* could just possibly have outfought the four armoured cruisers and Troubridge tamely declined action. *Goeben* and *Berslau* continued their voyage undisturbed, arrived safely and were incorporated with their crews into the Turkish Navy. Their bold action successfully convinced Turkey to join the war on the side of the Central Powers.

There could scarcely have been a more disastrous outcome for Britain.

Determined to avenge this shameful debacle the Royal Navy threw its full weight behind the third scheme for making use of their naval supremacy, this time by outflanking their enemies by means of an attack on Constantinople. The great guns of the battleships would be used to smash the Turkish forts and gun positions in the Dardanelles and the fleet would steam grandly up to the city, cow its inhabitants into submission and then threaten the southern flank of the Central Powers by sending a force up through Bulgaria, it would then attack the Austrian forces in the Balkans, and to reinforce the Russian's left flank. *Goeben* and *Breslau* would be captured skulking in a Turkish dockyard. Seldom can there have been a more ill-conceived strategy. Churchill however, backed by every naval officer determined to show that he was made of sterner stuff than Arky-Barky and Troubridge, adopted the scheme enthusiastically. The First Sea Lord, Jacky Fisher, immediately saw the dangers – the waters were narrow and intensively mined – how on earth was a naval expedition going to control a vast alien city? – was it realistic to think of sending soldiers northward from Asiatic Turkey to attack Austria when the British and French armies were likely to be hard pressed on the western front? All these objections were swept aside by Churchill's forceful personality and the ill-fated Dardanelles campaign was approved in London and in Paris.

The three schemes for making use of the overwhelming power of the Royal Navy all had one factor in common. They required ships mounting big guns which could be deployed in mine infested waters. These ships should have a shallow draft so as to be able to get close inshore and be proof against mines and torpedoes as far as possible, at the same time they must be able to be constructed, maintained and manned without diminishing the power of the Grand Fleet, or of the lighter forces on the east coast and at Dover, on which

Britain's safety depended. They must be cheap, easy to build quickly, preferably in yards not concerned with building conventional warships, and require only small crews.

Thus the concept of the monitor, a direct descendent of the bomb ketch, was born.

Chapter 2

Building the Monitors

Somewhat to its surprise the Admiralty found there were ships very roughly answering the requirements of monitors available for immediate purchase. (See drawing 1) The Brazilian Navy had decided that it required some heavily armed monitors of about 1,500 tons to work on its river system, especially on the River Amazon. An order was placed with Vickers of Barrow for three such vessels in 1912 and the ships completed their trials in December 1913 and were made ready for the voyage across the Atlantic. There was a problem however, in that the Brazilians had been hit by a decline in the price of their main export, rubber, due to the fact that seeds from rubber trees had been smuggled out of the country and found to flourish in British controlled Malaya. The unfortunate Brazilians suddenly found that they could not pay for their monitors. The ships were held in dock at Barrow and Vickers eagerly sought to find a buyer to replace their newly impoverished customers. The little ships were, however, so strange that no one could be found who was prepared to pay for them. Just before war broke out the Admiralty, luckily for Vickers, became concerned about a number of warships being built in British yards for foreign powers – there was a battleship and destroyers for Turkey for example, destroyers for Greece, and destroyers and battle-ships for Chile – all of whose attitude in the impending war was anything but certain – so the British Government took the decision to take all these ships over to prevent them from falling into the hands of potential enemies. At the same time they could place some powerful new vessels into the hands of the Royal Navy. The Brazilian monitors were included in the deal, not because the navy particularly wanted them but to prevent them from somehow falling into the wrong hands.

It is easy to understand why the Brazilian gun boats were unwanted (see drawing 1). They cost £155,000 each – a little more than a contemporary destroyer (For the sake of comparison, a *Queen Elizabeth* class fast battleship cost about £4m) and mounted two 6 inch guns in a single forward facing Vickers turret. (For comparative purposes it is worth remembering that the classic French field artillery piece the "Seventy five" threw a shell of about 12 pounds, the latest British M class destroyers had 4 inch guns with shells of 25 – 30 pounds, the 6 inch guns of the monitors fired 100 pound shells – they were thus far more formidable than any field artillery). There was also very powerful secondary armament in the form of two 4.7 inch howitzers, both on the after deck – ideal for riverine bombardment work – and four 3 pounders and six machine guns for self-protection. Unlike destroyers, they had quite heavy protective armour (¾ – 1 inch deck; 2 inch over magazines; 1½ – 3 inch side belt; 4 inch turret faces). This all made them quite effective floating gun platforms, but gun platforms strictly for river work, not for the open sea. For propulsion they had 1,450 horsepower triple expansion engines with dual fired (oil and coal) boilers giving them about 12 knots in still water. They had extremely shallow draft, only 4 foot 9 inches, and just 1 foot 6 inches freeboard, so that in anything approaching a seaway the whole deck was constantly awash. To achieve their shallow draft and carry their 1,250 ton weight they had to be extremely beamy, being 49 feet wide and 267 feet long, giving a length/beam ratio of 5.4:1, as against 10:1 for a typical destroyer. The two propellers were 5 foot 7 inches in diameter, 10 inches more than their draft, so they had to be housed in tunnels under the hull. This at first made the ships impossible to control astern, a problem which had to be overcome by fitting larger twin rudders and a flap over the stern to control the water flow to the propellers. Altogether they were a seaman's nightmare, underpowered, unhandy and unable to cope with heavy seas. They did have one feature which raised a wry smile with their officers. The standard of luxury demanded by the Brazilian Navy was incredibly high, the cabins and messes were beautifully finished in polished tropical woods and the leather covered furniture might have graced the first class lounge of the proudest ocean liner.

The captains selected for these strange vessels were Commander Fullerton (*Severn*) Lieutenant Commander Wilson (*Mersey*) and Commander Snagge (*Humber*). Officers were a mixture of regulars from the Royal Naval Reserve and Royal Naval Volunteer Reserve and the seamen were all reservists.

When the three monitors were commissioned into British service their shortcomings soon became evident. They were sluggish, impossible to control in a crosswind, very difficult to make go astern and abominably wet. Indeed *Humber* was almost swamped when at anchor just outside the harbour mouth. They were obviously unsuitable for service with the Grand Fleet but it was thought that, until one or other of the outflanking schemes was authorised, they might be useful to the Dover Patrol. Off they set for Dover from Barrow, only to encounter a strong gale in the Irish Sea. Waves soon washed over the decks and water came in through the ventilators and hatches, flooding the crew's quarters and threatening to reach the engine rooms. The crew had to be accommodated in the officer's quarters throughout the voyage as their own remained awash. The strong winds made the flat bottomed hulls skid sideways and they wallowed horribly in the swells. It was a severe ordeal for the crews and showed clearly that river boats, however excellent for their intended purpose, are not safe at sea. To add insult to injury, they looked so strange that they were almost fired on twice by coastal guns, and were held under arrest off Dover by the guard ship who mistook them for some strange enemy intruders. All three did eventually arrive at Dover however and there they were to do sterling service as we shall see later.

These little ships lacked the underwater protection, the ammunition capacity and the fire power of later monitors, also the weather often caused them to have to cease operations and head for shelter, but they were to prove most useful ships, performing feats which would be impossible for any other type of vessel. Their success caused the Admiralty to take a favourable view of the monitor as a type and plan for more ambitious variations on the same theme.

As well as these Brazilians, two other unusual ships were fitting out in Britain in 1914 (see figure 2). The Norwegian Government had a requirement for coastal defence vessels and had had two of them built by Armstrong Whitworth early in the century. Two more were ordered in 1913 and these had already been launched when the war broke out. The Admiralty immediately set out to purchase them and eventually a price of £370,000 each was agreed. In contrast to the river monitors these were not unlike small battleships and were proper sea boats of 4,800 tons (increased to 5,800 by the time they were completed). They were quite heavily armed with two 9.45 inch guns in turrets as main armament and two 5.9 inch super firing in turrets mounted over the top of the 9.45 inchers. They also each had two torpedo tubes. The citadels were protected by 7 inches of protective armour and there was a 2 inch protective deck covering the whole length of the ships. Twin 2,000 horsepower triple expansion engines with dual fuel boilers gave a design speed of 15 knots. Unfortunately their gun sizes did not conform to standard British ammunition, and the guns had to be removed and re-bored to take standard 9.2 inch and 6 inch shells. A most unusual feature of the modified turrets was the potential to elevate the main armament up to 40 degrees, and using special charges a maximum range of 39,000 yards (22 miles) was obtained, slightly greater than the range of the 15 inch armament fitted to the most powerful battleships. (Note: this was useful for shore bombardment but there was little possibility of hitting an enemy ship at anything like this distance. The longest range hit ever made on a moving ship was achieved by the 15 inch battleship *Warspite* on the Italian *Julio Cesare* at a range of about 15 miles – (26,400 yards) during the Second World War). The modifications to the guns and other work specified by the Admiralty to fit the ships for Royal Navy use such as fitting anti-torpedo bulges under water, improving the accommodation and changes to the secondary armament, held up final completion of these ships. Their place in the queue at the builders was also continually taken by work considered to be more urgent, so it was not until 1918 that they finally sailed to join the Dover Patrol. They had been named *Glatton* and *Gorgon*. *Gorgon*'s wartime history is related in a subsequent chapter but *Glatton*'s tragic end came almost as soon as she was commissioned.

Admiral Roger Keyes commanding the Dover Patrol had been glad when his friend Commander Neston Diggle arrived at Dover with his new ship *Glatton,* in time to join the bombardment of the Belgian coast. The admiral invited his friend for tea with his family and they were walking on the cliffs together when a terrific explosion shook Dover and a black mushroom cloud erupted from somewhere near the harbour. The two men rushed back to the admiral's house where they were informed by telephone that *Glatton* had experienced an explosion in one of her magazines and was on fire. Jumping into the admiral's wife's old Ford they were driven at breakneck speed to the harbour to find an operation already in hand to evacuate many terribly burned people from *Glatton* and tugs alongside her pumping water into the fire. They also saw that in the next berth lay the ammunition ship *Gransha*. *Gransha* had enough ammunition aboard to devastate the whole of Dover. Diggle found that the only surviving officer on board his ship was a junior surgeon who was busy with the wounded, but a petty officer on shore leave came on board and joined the captain in a desperate search for the seacocks and the flooding keys for the magazines. They managed to flood the forward part of the ship but the after part could not be reached through the still raging fire and it was only a question of time before the aft magazine blew up, probably taking *Gransha* and most of Dover with it. To make matters worse there were many men below crying out for help and seamen from nearby ships had swarmed on board to try to save them. After about forty-five terrible minutes the cries from below ceased and the admiral ordered the ship to be abandoned and sunk to put out the fires.

Keyes at once went on board the nearest destroyer and ordered her to manoeuvre to torpedo the blazing hulk, but she did not have steam up. Disgusted, he transferred to another destroyer and told the captain to get close to *Glatton* and sink her. To do this the little propeller on the front of the torpedo, which was intended to prevent it from exploding too close to the ship firing it, had to be disabled, and although the captain ordered this to be done it was not, so the torpedo struck the side of the hull of *Glatton* but did not explode. Keyes was now in a "fever of impatience" as he called it. Well he might be in the circumstances. Another torpedo was fired, this time successfully, and it blew a great hole in the *Glatton*'s side. Keyes wanted the ship to sink on an even keel and ordered a third torpedo to be fired from the other side of her. When he got into the firing position however he realised that the missile might pass clean under the ship and hit other vessels in the harbour. He therefore returned to his original position and put the third torpedo through the hole made by the second. This did the trick and *Glatton* sunk safely to the bottom of the harbour. Sixty men had been killed and 124 seriously injured. Nineteen of the injured died soon afterwards. The remains of *Glatton* still lie, buried in sand, just outside Dover Harbour.

There was an immediate enquiry as to what had caused this disaster. A similar incident had occurred in 1915 when the minelayer *Princess Irene* had exploded at Sheerness with the loss of all hands, the accident being attributed to a faulty fuse. In *Glatton*'s case enemy action was quickly ruled out, and stories of spies and sabotage which abounded at first, were quickly discounted. A close examination of procedures on board established the alarming fact that hot cinders from the boilers were routinely piled against the magazine bulkhead. The bulkhead was made of steel plates backed by granulated cork and timber. Experiments on *Gorgon* showed that the temperature in the magazine could be made to rise to up to 150 degrees Fahrenheit by piling cinders against the bulkhead, but this was not nearly hot enough to ignite the magazine. Cork at this temperature however could give off an inflammable gas, and the court of enquiry concluded that this was to blame for the explosion. Operating procedures in *Gorgon* were revised and work set in hand to replace the cork. While this was in progress a more likely cause of the explosion came to light. Engineers found that several rivets had been left out of the steel plating in *Gorgon*'s bulkheads, and also that instead of cork, old newspapers had been stuffed into the insulation space when the ship was being fitted out. They concluded that in *Glatton*'s case these had caught fire and the fire had been fanned by air coming in through the empty rivet holes. The enquiry was not re-opened but there is not much doubt that the tragedy was the result of this carelessness in the shipyard.

When the battleship *Audacious* was mined in October 1914 the liner *Olympic*, a sister ship to *Titanic*, attempted to tow her and to pick up survivors. The navy was desperate to keep the news of *Audacious*'s loss secret and so all the passengers from *Olympic* were detained as soon as she docked. All, that is, but one. Admiral Sir John Jellicoe, commander of the Grand Fleet, interviewed a first class passenger, Mr Charles Schwab, President of the Bethlehem Steel Corporation, and found that he had an appointment in London with Lord Kitchener, and was hoping for an order to build submarines and other armaments for Britain, Bethlehem also had four 14 inch gun turrets in the factory almost complete and ready to be delivered to a German yard for installation on a battle cruiser being built for Greece. The turrets could not be delivered however because of the British blockade. Would the Admiralty like to make an offer? Jellicoe was impressed and Schwab was released and rushed to London. Turrets were the most complex part of a large warship and capacity to build them was limited. If the Admiralty wanted heavy gun monitors for coastal bombardment, here was their chance. Churchill and Fisher jumped at the opportunity. Four 14 inch monitors, *Abercrombie, Havelock, Raglan* and *Roberts* were set in hand in November 1914 (see drawing 3).

From the outset the design of the ships was rushed and inadequate. At first glance the requirements seemed simple. What was needed was a barge-like hull, drawing not more than 10 feet of water, on which would be mounted a single turret, which with its ammunition would weigh about 1,000 tons. A modest speed of around 10 knots would be adequate. Altogether it seemed a pretty simple proposition. As the project grew, however, so did the complications. The ships would need protection against torpedoes and mines. The Director of Naval Construction, Tennyson d'Eyncourt, had designed a system for doing just this. It consisted of an enormous bulge under water along the whole length of each of the ship's sides. Inside, the bulge was divided into two compartments, the outer one, 10 feet wide, was air filled and water tight and the inner one was 5 feet wide and open to the sea (see drawing 2). A torpedo or mine striking the ship would explode against the outer part of the bulge, well clear of vulnerable parts of the ship. Splinters and shock waves from the explosion would be further dissipated in the water filled inboard compartment. Anti-mine wires would be fitted outside the bulges to provide additional protection. These bulges were added to the monitor's hulls. To guard against gunfire the citadel was protected by 4 inches of armour and both the upper and lower decks were armoured to protect against bombs or high trajectory shells. All this extra weight resulted in a ship of 6,150 tons, 334 feet long and 90 feet wide, with a draft of only 10 feet – hardly the lines of a speedy vessel. Each ship cost about £550,000.

The real problem came with the propulsion system. All four ships had two steam piston engines driving twin screws and were coal fired. They had Babcock water tube boilers. *Abercrombie* and *Havelock* had quadruple expansion engines, *Raglan* had four cylinder triple expansion engines and *Roberts* three cylinder triple expansion units which were to prove to be the least satisfactory of all. The hull form was such that only two fairly small propellers could be fitted, and water flow to these was masked by the shape of the bulges. Unfortunately the engines had to be specified and ordered before any tests on hull models could be completed and as a result the ships were built with 1,800 horsepower instead of the 4-5,000 horsepower which the model tests indicated would be required to achieve 10 knots. The results were predictable. On trials the ships achieved a little over 6 knots. The propellers were changed and the mine wires removed, but still they struggled to get near 7 knots on trials in still water. This would be hardly enough to move them against the tide in the Dover Strait with a head wind. *Roberts,* the slowest of the slow, only managed 5.7 knots in flat water. It was also found that foul weather and a crosswind made them crab sideways so that their track through the water could often be 45 degrees different to the ship's head. Any long sea voyage demanded that they should be towed. On

one occasion the captain of *Roberts* rigged a foresail and a
mizzen staysail to try to push his ship a bit faster. With this
rig combined with the efforts of her own engines and a tug
she only managed 3.5 knots in a Biscay gale.

The deck layout was quite simple. There was an armoured
conning tower on the foredeck, beneath the barrels of the
massive American 14 inch turret. (Conning towers were a
feature of many warships of the period. They were abandoned when it became clear that poor visibility and general
inconvenience made them a serious disadvantage). Aft of the
turret was a substantial tripod mast with a compass platform,
a spotting top, gun-director station and 9 foot range finder.
Behind the funnel there were derricks and accommodation
for two seaplanes which were to be used for spotting. In
practice these were seldom embarked, partly because they
tended to be damaged by the blast and recoil of the great
guns, so had to be unloaded and towed when the guns were
likely to be fired.

As floating gun platforms the ships were reasonably satisfactory. The broad hulls gave excellent stability. Unlike most
British turrets, which were hydraulically powered, these US
built units were electrically powered by two 200 kilowatt
steam driven generators. In practice they worked quite well
once the crews got used to them. Guns were aimed from the
director tower which sent elevation and directional instructions to the layers in the turret. Maximum gun elevation was
only 15 degrees, which was fine for a battle cruiser, designed
for ship to ship combat, but not really enough for shore
bombardment. Maximum range was 19,900 yards (11.3
miles) – much less than the 9.2 inch guns of *Glatton* and
Gorgon. In practice the ships were often heeled over when
firing at distant targets so as to increase effective gun eleva-

tion. Secondary armament consisted of four 3 inch 12 pounders to ward off torpedo boats. It was correctly anticipated that these ships would often be in a situation where they would be in range of enemy airships and aeroplanes so they were fitted with 3 pounder anti-aircraft guns and 2 pounder pom-poms.

Accommodation for the crew of 189 (twelve officers, 177 men) was quite Spartan, the ships being designed, as instructed by Fisher, "with no fah la lah's". The crews were more comfortable in a seaway, however, than their mates in more conventional ships: although the monitors were so slow and clumsy, they were very stable in rough weather and rolled much less than cruisers or even battleships.

One of the prime requirements of the 14 inch monitors was that they should be available quickly. Fisher and Churchill were both aching to get their hands on them for their various projects off the north German coast and in the Dardanelles. Rushed design and construction was indeed the root cause of their major shortcomings. One of the challenges facing the Admiralty when the monitor concept was approved was to find yards with capacity to build such beamy ships immediately. In the end two, *Havelock* and *Abercrombie,* were built at Harland and Wolff in Belfast, taking the place of a liner no longer required due to the outbreak of war. One ship, *Raglan,* was built at the same company's Govan yard. The fourth, *Roberts* was constructed at Wallsend by Swan Hunter. Build time was indeed very quick. The ships were laid down in December 1914, launched in April/May 1915 and completed a month later. Oddly the ships changed their names almost as soon as they were built. Originally Churchill had had them named after famous American generals and admirals as a gesture of thanks for the delivery of the guns. To his surprise the Americans objected strongly as they wished to preserve their strict neutral status, so the names had to be hurriedly painted out and British generals put in their place.

In service these ponderous vessels underwent a few modifications. The conning tower was not a satisfactory position for the navigating officer who, in the absence of a proper bridge, normally worked from the searchlight station half way up the mast. With a following wind however this position was completely obscured by smoke from the funnel. To reduce this, taller funnels were fitted to all these ships, and at the same time the searchlight platform was given some weather protection. The only other major changes were the removal of the aeroplane hangar and handling equipment, its place being taken by a 6 inch gun, used for driving off enemy destroyers or surfaced submarines. Enhanced anti-aircraft armament of various sorts was also fitted.

The 14 inch monitors did not mark the end of Churchill's and Fisher's quest for a shallow draft bombardment fleet. Both men still clung to the hope that the navy might make a landing on the German coast, even Churchill, whose mind was becoming ever more focused on the idea of the Dardanelles project, did not abandon the idea of an amphibious assault on German territory as well. Before the 14 inch ships could be launched the two men turned their attention to another project, this time involving disarming some obsolete battleships and mounting their guns on a new series of monitors. Unfortunately once again pressure to get the ships built quickly meant that almost no lessons could be learnt from the four 14 inch vessels.

The *Majestic* class of battleships had been commenced in 1893. They were fine looking vessels with black hulls, white upper-works and yellow masts and funnels. They had four

12 inch guns in two turrets. Having been designed long before the revolutionary *Dreadnought* they were pitifully slow, with a top speed of only 17 knots, and had poor protection against guns or underwater weapons. Obviously they could not form a part of the Grand Fleet. The turrets however were known to be well designed and the Admiralty decided that if these could be removed and placed on a shallow draft hull with good underwater protection they could have a new life as main armament for monitors. Accordingly four of the nine Majestics were disarmed to allow the construction of eight monitors, *Lord Clive, Prince Rupert, Sir John Moore, General Crauford, Prince Eugine, The Earl of Peterborough, Sir Thomas Picton* and *General Wolfe* (see drawing 4).

These eight ships were commenced well before the launch of the 14 inch monitors and they were built with similar hulls and hence many of the same shortcomings. As the turrets already existed the cost of the ships was much less than their predecessors, being about £260,000 each. They displaced 5,900 tons, slightly less than the 14 inch ships. One of the first considerations was to extend the range of the guns by giving them more elevation. A 13.5 degree elevation was all that was required on the old battleships, giving a range of 13,700 yards, however the makers (Elswick) considered that the elevation could readily be increased to 30 degrees which would give 21,000 yards. It took much longer than expected to get the guns to work properly at high angles of elevation, but eventually the difficulties were overcome. The ships had the usual collection of close defence and anti-aircraft armament.

Once again the weakness was in the propulsion system. Fisher was an enthusiast for diesel engines because of their fuel economy, especially at cruising speed. He tried hard to get them fitted to these monitors. He hated coal firing and was impressed by the potential of diesels as a replacement for oil fired steam turbines in low speed vessels. It was impossible, however, to build large internal combustion engines in the time available, also the navy had no experience of diesel propulsion and indeed the technology was in its infancy. In the end they had to settle for triple expansion three cylinder, or in some cases four cylinder, steam engines with coal fired boilers. Engines were slightly different in different ships, but they were all more powerful than those in the 14 inch monitors with an average of about 2,400 horse-power giving them a trials speed of about 7.5 knots – still pitifully slow for working in tidal waters.

As usual the work of constructing the ships was spread over a number of builders, five were contracted to Harland and Wolff, and one each to Scotts, Hamiltons and Fairfields. Construction was impressively rapid, orders being placed in December 1914 and the ships being commissioned between June and October of 1915.

In service these ships, most of which were to be employed in the Dover Strait and off the Belgian coast, underwent some astonishing modifications. Six inch guns were quickly provided to give protection from enemy destroyer attacks and anti-aircraft armament was steadily increased, at the same time Maxim guns were fitted to give protection from remote control motorboats. This all led to a requirement for a larger crew and more accommodation which was provided by enclosing some of the open deck space. Large smoke generators were fitted to give protection from shore batteries. Most astonishing of all, three ships, *Lord Clive, Prince Eugene* and *General Wolfe,* were equipped with the largest guns ever mounted on a British warship. Each was fitted in 1918 with an 18 inch single turret weighing, with its ammunition and supports, over 700 tons. This massive gun was installed on the after deck so that the original 12 inch main armament could be retained on the foredeck. The extra weight aft made the stern very deep in the water, which was partially counteracted by emptying the inner section of the anti-torpedo bulge of water. Even so the draft aft was increased from 9 foot 10 inches to 13 foot 2 inches. As this put the bulge well under water, leaving a large unprotected section of hull exposed, a heavy steel structure had to be added to fend off remote-controlled boats. The 18 inch guns and turrets had originally been intended for the cruisers *Furious* and *Courageous*, which were eventually completed as aircraft carriers. The 18 inch guns had then been modified for possible use ashore for very long range bombardment and were of a unique design, they could only be fired at elevations of 22 to 45 degrees, giving a range at maximum elevation of 40,000 yards (22.7 miles), throwing a projectile weighing 1.5 tons at a velocity of 2,300 feet per second (1,568 mph). The recoil of these massive weapons would force the ship violently sideways, and it is astonishing that the structure was able to stand up to the shock loading. They were pointed over the side of the ship and could only traverse 10 degrees each side of their centre line, so coarse aiming had to be done by swinging the ship, using anchors. Fortunately for the German forces in Belgium the 18 inch armament was not ready in time to be used more than briefly in September 1918. The only other ships ever built using guns this size were the spectacularly unsuccessful Japanese *Yamato* class battleships of the Second World War.

The "Generals" as the 12 inch monitors were collectively christened, did not mark the end of the rush to build Fisher's shallow-draft fleet. After the Battle of the Falkland Islands

(7 December 1914) the Admiralty decided that very high speed was an essential requirement for battle cruisers, and so the two new ships being built at that time, *Renown* and *Repulse,* were redesigned leaving out two of their 15 inch turrets to reduce weight and increase speed to 32 knots. Eight turrets, four for each ship, however had already been ordered and so two of them from each ship became redundant. Fisher immediately snapped these up for two new especially powerful monitors. (In the event they were not the actual guns fitted, changing priorities in the Grand Fleet meant that it was more convenient to fit the almost identical 15 inch turrets intended for *Royal Sovereign* class battleships to the monitors and use those from the battle cruisers elsewhere). The 15 inch Mark 1 gun had been developed by the Elswick Ordinance Company of Newcastle for the *Queen Elizabeth* class fast battleships. It was an excellent weapon which gave good service through two world wars. Indeed the last British battleship ever built, *Vanguard* which entered service in 1946, was fitted with a slightly modified version of this same turret. The two new 15 inch monitors were named *Marshal Ney* and *Marshal Soult* after the celebrated Napoleonic generals (see drawing 5). This time the names, chosen to honour Britain's allies, were a source of delight, French officers visiting *Ney* exclaimed cried out, enraptured "Ah, le plus brave des braves."

Once again the rush to build these two new ships meant that they were designed before the first 14 inch monitors had been tested and their weaknesses uncovered. To make matters even worse the Admiralty actually found two sets of diesel engines with which to power them. Before the war two fleet oilers had been ordered and it had been decided to fit them each with two 750 horsepower diesels to test the tech-

nology. These engines Fisher snaffeled for his two 15 inch
monitors. One pair of engines, fitted to *Marshal Ney* were six-
cylinder two strokes designed by a German company, MAN.
They were actually assembled by Samuel White of Cowes.
The other pair, fitted to *Marshal Soult,* were eight-cylinder
four strokes designed and built by Vickers. Once again the
hull design followed the unsatisfactory lines of the first monitors and the ships were pitifully underpowered, making only
about 6 knots flat out in still water. The engines did deliver
much better fuel economy than steam engines fitted to
previous monitors (about 0.6 tons/hour). Diesels, however,
brought with them a new set of problems which did not occur
with steam engines, reliability. From the start the Vickers
engines worked quite well, but the MAN's fitted to *Ney* were
a nightmare. They stopped for no apparent reason whenever
load or speed was changed. They refused to run astern when
required to do so. (Like most marine diesels they had no
reversing gears, the engine was stopped and re-started back-
wards). Once stopped, they would be impossible to re-start,
the supply of air bottles used to crank the engines becoming
rapidly exhausted. On one occasion a fleet bombarding the
Belgian coast witnessed the extraordinary sight of this 6,900
ton monitor being towed out of the action with her two 750
horsepower engines both broken down, by the 900 ton
destroyer *Viking* going slow ahead with her 15,000 horsepower steam turbines. While thus being towed she made a
good 10 knots – almost twice her normal full speed. *Soult's*
engines worked well, but unfortunately her propellers were
the wrong size for the 150 RPM of the engines. This made her
even slower than *Ney,* but at least she was reliable. The correct
propellers were eventually fitted and increased her speed by
a little less than half a knot, to about 6.6 knots in still water.

Once again speed of construction was impressive. The ships were ordered in January 1915 and the first, *Ney*, launched in August. When launched the new ships displaced 6,900 tons and cost £270,000 each excluding the turrets.

The "Marshals" as these ungainly ships were called had other shortcomings. The very high turret was too close to the compass platform, so the compass needle would invariably swing round, following the gun. The steering was appalling, the steering engines being too small and the rudders insufficient, probably the windage of the turret on top of its 20 foot high column was partly responsible for the bad handling characteristics. Ships berthed near them in harbour mostly showed the scars resulting from their clumsy manoeuvres. In strong winds the ships could not be controlled at all, skidding sideways and sometimes making a complete circle, regardless of the rudder. In practice they needed a tow for any long voyage.

Soult was in action from her launch date for the duration of the war, but underwent some extensive modification. The conning tower was removed and a bridge built aft of the funnel. The funnel itself was lengthened and the mast modified to take two huge searchlights and a revised navigator's station. The main armament was modified to give 30 degrees of elevation in place of the original 20, thus increasing the range from 26,000 yards to about 32,000 yards (18.2 miles). At the same time extra defensive armament in the form of eight 4-inch guns and anti-aircraft armament was added. The result was to make an already ugly ship certainly the most ill-looking vessel in the navy. She remained slow and ungainly but was a good gun platform, and rendered, as we shall see, some useful service. She was still afloat in 1939 and consideration was given to bringing her back into service, but the plan was abandoned. *Ney* was so clumsy and unreliable that her main armament was removed and she was relegated to guard ship duties for which she was given a complement of 6-inch guns.

The next batch of large monitors was to be an altogether different proposition (see drawing 6). By mid 1915 it was obvious that the performance of all the fourteen large ships already ordered was going to be well short of requirements especially as regards speed and handling at sea. In May 1915 four new monitors with 15-inch guns were provisionally ordered, only to be cancelled when it became clear that guns and turrets could not be supplied without an unacceptable delay in the completion of the *Royal Oak* class of battleships. It then became apparent that the Marshalls (*Ney* and *Soult*) were going to perform even worse than their predecessors, and it was determined that entirely new hulls should be designed, giving a much slimmer more easily driven form, with the screws able to operate efficiently, unobstructed by the bulges in the hull. These new monitors would be equipped with much more powerful engines and the turrets of the disgraced Marshals would be mounted on them. So began the story of *Erebus* and *Terror*, which were both to prove very formidable warships.

To achieve better hydrodynamic shape the hulls were lengthened and the anti-torpedo bulges made slimmer. This was achieved by replacing the inner chamber of the bulge, which on previous ships had been open to the sea, by a narrower space filled with sealed steel tubes, the crushing of which would absorb much of the energy of any explosion. Unlike the earlier monitors in which the bulges had been awash, the new ships had theirs projecting 15 inches above the waterline. This made them even more stable and greatly eased the handling of the ship's boats. The resulting hulls were 405 feet long by 88 foot 2 inches broad as against 355 feet 8 inches and 90 foot 3 inches for the Marshals. Critically the stern sections were much finer giving far better water flow to the propellers. There was a single large rudder. A secondary bow rudder for manoeuvring and for going astern was proposed but not fitted, this bow rudder was proposed at the suggestion of the Dover Patrol, whose experience in bombarding the Belgian coast suggested that it would be useful to be able to deploy the full weight of the ship's firepower while backing away from the enemy coast. Most important of all, the inadequate engines of previous monitors were replaced by two four-cylinder triple expansion oil-fired steam engines of 3,000 horsepower each, four times the power of the Marshal's diesels. Armament was similar to their predecessors, with two 15 inch, two 6 inch and two 12-pounder guns plus the usual complement of anti-aircraft weapons. The turrets themselves were not in the end taken from *Soult* as she was proving too useful to take out of service, so *Terror* used *Ney*'s 15 inch main armament whilst *Erebus* received a brand new reserve turret originally allocated to the battle cruiser *Furious*.(*Furious* was designed to have 18 inch guns but a back-up set of 15 inch had been built in case the 18 inch weapons proved unsatisfactory. She was eventually completed as an aircraft carrier with no heavy armament at all). Both sets of guns were modified before fitting to the monitors to have a maximum elevation of 30 degrees which gave them an extra 6,000 yards range (bringing it up to 32,000 yards or 18.2 miles). Armour protection was similar to that in the previous ships. There was a proper bridge in place of the inadequate conning tower arrangement and a tall funnel aft of it, so the ships at last looked like proper warships. The extra machinery weight meant that draft was increased by a little over 1 foot to 11 foot 8 inches.

The results of the design changes and the greater power were apparent as soon as the ships were first tried, in August 1916. While the previous monitors had never achieved anything like their design speed of 10 knots, the new ships comfortably exceeded the 12 knot maximum which had been expected of them, *Erebus* making over 14 knots on trials and *Terror* just over 13 knots. With their extra draft and finer lines the ships initially handled reasonably well in a seaway and the engines proved very reliable. Handiness was much reduced however during the 1940s, especially for *Erebus*, when a plethora of new equipment, including radars, extra accommodation, increased anti-aircraft armament and a large mizzen mast, were fitted. All this "clobber" increased draft by almost 2 feet and caused so much windage aft that a foresail had the be resorted in order to make the ship possible to handle in strong winds. It was rigged either on the fore-mast or on one of the gun barrels at maximum elevation. Without it she would stubbornly point upwind whatever the steersman did with the rudder. Surely this was the last example of a sail being used on a British warship.

These two ships, being more complicated and requiring modifications to their turrets to achieve the extra range, took longer to build than their predecessors, just under a year from commencement to completion. They cost a little under £400,000 each excluding the cost of the main armament, which was scavenged from other projects.

There was one further class of monitor built for service in the First World War (see drawing 7). By early 1915 the Gallipoli campaign was under way and shallow draft heavy gun vessels would clearly be extremely useful in this theatre, also it had become obvious that many of the old protected cruisers being used as patrol vessels enforcing the blockade of Germany were simply not up to the job. They were too slow, too vulnerable and insufficiently reliable. They were also much too slow to operate with the Grand Fleet. Their patrol duties were taken over by more modern light cruisers and destroyers, assisted by armed merchant vessels. The 9.2 inch guns of the old cruisers, however, were serviceable and could form the main armament of a new family of small monitors. These weapons had a useful maximum elevation of 30 degrees and a range of 25,000 yards (16,000 in the case of some of the oldest turrets). At the same time a number of 6 inch turrets mounted on old battleships became redundant, and these could be used in pairs on similar small ships. Hence plans were made for nineteen small monitors, which were unnamed, being known only as M15 to M33.

These were simple ships, built to commercial shipbuilding standards, without protective bulges and with very little defensive armour. They were 171 feet long and 31 feet broad with a draft of only 6 feet for the 6 inch armed ships and 7 feet for the 9.2s. Displacement was between 580 and 650 tons. Once again Fisher wanted diesels and this time eight of the ships were fitted with Swedish Bolinder semi-diesel engines. These were quite widely used commercial engines and proved tough and reliable. Different combinations of engines were used in different ships depending on availability, some driving two screws and some driving four. Power varied from 560 to 640 break horsepower. Semi-diesels had lower compression ratios than conventional diesels so that stresses on moving parts were reduced, the fuel was ignited in an electrically heated space by a combination of heat and pressure. Remarkably one ship, *M24*, had four cylinder paraffin engines built by the Campbell Gas Engine Company of Halifax. The only major fault found with the diesel ships was a tendency for soot and un-burnt fuel to catch fire in the funnel, sometimes with alarming consequences. The other small monitors had conventional triple expansion steam engines, all being oil burning. These small monitors were reasonable sea boats and could achieve a little under 10 knots in trials. One of them *M33,* renamed *Minerva,* is the only monitor still in existence, being preserved in dry dock at Portsmouth, complete with her two 6 inch guns (2011) It will take little imagination on the part of any visitor to comprehend the harsh living conditions endured by the crew in their comfortless steel box..

Being constructed to commercial, as opposed to naval, standards, they were quite cheap at £35-40,000 per ship, excluding the cost of the "second hand" main armament. During the course of the war changes were made to the armament of some of these ships. Since the 9.2s were not suitable for bombarding the heavily defended Belgian coast, they were dismounted to be used as land based artillery. They were replaced on the monitors by 6 inch or sometimes 7.5 inch guns, again scavenged from older ships. As usual the secondary armament underwent many changes with emphasis on anti-aircraft capability.

As we shall see these little ships had an active war in many spheres and proved extremely useful both in the shore bombardment role and as heavily armed patrol ships, keeping enemy destroyers away from net defences and minefields. Four of them were lost during the war due to enemy activity between 1915 and 1919, (others were wrecked or deliberately scuttled for various reasons), but many survived in civilian or auxiliary military use for many years, for example, eight were converted into small oil tankers and used by Shell in South America, and one was used by the Royal Navy as a torpedo training vessel.

Astonishingly 1918 did not see the end of British monitor building. Churchill, who was First Lord of the Admiralty in 1939 immediately tried to re-activate the monitor fleet, with the idea of repeating the harassment of German armies moving along the Belgian coast, using the same tactic that was deployed in 1914-18. *Erebus* and *Terror* were still in service, although they needed improved deck armour and anti-aircraft armament before they could be risked in combat close to enemy coasts. They were therefore not available until after the blitzkrieg had swept away the French and Belgian armies but, as we shall see, played an important role in other theatres. *Soult* was still afloat but in such a condition that she would be uneconomic to bring into active service. Her gun turret however was still in good order. The decision was taken to use this and another redundant 15 inch turret in two new monitors, *Roberts* and *Abercrombie* (see drawing 8). They were supposed to follow the same general design and layout as *Erebus* and *Terror* but with enhanced deck armour, a modern radar fit and formidable anti-aircraft capability.

In practice the new ships differed considerably from their predecessors. Instead of steam piston engines, diesels were at first selected, but as none of the required power was immediately available, steam turbines were eventually installed. A speed of 15 knots was originally specified, but calculations showed that this would require at least 11,000 horsepower and too much space would be needed for machinery. The turbines fitted produced 4,800 horsepower giving just over 12 knots. The protective bulge in the hulls was to a new design, evolved from extensive testing of various underwater protection arrangements carried out between the wars. There were three compartments, an outer air-filled space, then a centre space filled with water. The inner space was air filled and backed by a thick armoured hull. The idea was that the mine or torpedo would explode as far from the hull as possible, and the outer air space would reduce the pressure pulse set up by the explosion. The water filled space would reduce the velocity of splinters and spread the force of the explosion over a wide area. The inner space prevented pressure waves from being transmitted to the armoured hull. Water tight compartments within the hull limited the possibility of flooding and a large circulation pump was provided to enable counter flooding of the air tight compartments so as to keep the ship on an even keel if she was damaged under water. *Roberts* was laid down in April 1940 and after various problems and delays completed in October 1942. *Abercrombie* was delayed by more urgent work at the Vickers Armstrong yard on the Tyne and was not commenced until May 1941 then there were further delays and modifications made to the anti-aircraft armament and radar fit so that she was not commissioned until May 1943. She might well have been abandoned altogether if *Terror* had not been sunk in February 1941. The long build periods of these ships compared to earlier monitors reflect the much greater sophistication of the design, machinery, secondary armament and electronics. *Roberts* had a Dreyer fire control system similar to that of *Erebus*. *Abercrombie* had a much superior electronic system and both ships had centrally controlled radar directed anti-aircraft armament with long range high altitude protection provided by 4 inch high angle quick-firing guns with close range protection provided by a variety of quick firers, pom-poms and machine guns.

Altogether these were well designed, effective ships, much better looking and more workmanlike than their predecessors. Every effort was made to give them sufficient anti-aircraft protection and this was to be vital in the roles they were designed to play, working close to enemy held coasts. As we shall see, even this was not always sufficient. Unfortunately with complexity comes cost. These ships cost over £1.1m each excluding armament and had an establishment of nineteen officers and 423 ratings. This was almost three times the cost of *Erebus* and *Terror* and roughly twice the complement. (The earlier ships cost £380,000 on the same basis and had a complement of 226 when first built).

Chapter 3

Monitors Enter Service

The first monitors to see active service with the Royal Navy were the three ex-Brazilian gun boats. They arrived at Dover on 28 August after their hazardous voyage down the Irish Sea. Almost immediately they were sent plodding off to Ostend to help to extricate the two naval divisions which Churchill had sent to attempt to protect the city, but they arrived off the town too late to take part in the evacuation. Their next mission was to assist in the evacuation of two army divisions from the area, but in the event these managed to break through by land to Mons. Next they were ordered to evacuate the Belgian court to Dunkirk. Again they arrived too late to be of any service and were then sent off to patrol the Thames Estuary, taking turns to go into dock to have improved armour plating mounted around the decks and magazines. On their way there *Severn* was attacked by a U-boat on the surface, she was saved by her shallow draft, the torpedo passing safely under her. To avoid another attack she steamed deliberately into a minefield, in the hope that the mines would be laid too deep for her to detonate them but would make the area impossibly dangerous for submarines. Luckily she was right.

The land war was meanwhile proceeding apace. The initial

German advance was halted by the Allies on the Marne, forcing the German high command to focus its efforts on trying to outflank the Allies by pressing westwards from their bases on the line Antwerp (which they captured on 9 October) – Gent – Bruges down the coast to take Ostend and Dunkirk. At the same time the Allies were seeking to probe the right flank of the German Army. The fighting on the sodden, flat, lands of the Belgian coast became savage and confused with horrendous casualties on both sides (see map 1). Eventually the Belgians managed to establish a defensive line on the River Yser, just east of Nieuwport. Both sides were running very short of heavy ammunition so that the artillery, which played such a vital role in all military operations, was strictly rationed and in some instances field guns actually had to be withdrawn from the battlefield for lack of ammunition supply. Urgent pleas for help reached the Royal Navy. The waters off the Belgian coast were beset with sandbanks and were threatened by German submarines, but it was vital to give the Belgian forces on land the cover of the heavy guns of the navy. A naval presence was also essential to guard against any possibility of a German amphibious assault behind the lines. *Severn, Humber* and *Mersey* were withdrawn from patrol in home waters, arriving to stand off Ostend on 10 October. Some troops were evacuated with their help as the town fell to the advancing Germans.

On 16 October bombardment in support of the rump of the Belgian Army was to begin in earnest off the Belgian coast, but rough weather prevented the monitors from sailing until the 18th. On this day the crazy little ships showed what they were made of. From 200 yards off the shore they harassed enemy troop movements on the road towards Nieuwport, then under heavy counter fire from German batteries ashore, they withdrew to 10,000 yards, out of range of the field guns, and continued with a steady and lethal bombardment. At one point a German battery being set up on the sand dunes was devastated by fire from *Severn*'s 4.7 inch howitzer. High sand dunes made spotting of fall of shot inland impossible for the officers on board the monitors, but there was radio contact with the Belgian Army HQ who at first directed fire by radio and flag signal, then sent an officer on board *Severn* to assist with communications. He was able to congratulate the monitors on their effective firing. They had, he said, killed 1,600 German soldiers including General von Tripp and his staff and destroyed six artillery pieces during their first day of action. How accurate this information was is open to question, but certainly the unexpected gunfire from the sea, enfilading the advancing German troops, had put new heart into the Belgian defenders. On the 20th the ships landed machine gun parties to help with the defence of the little town of Westende which nevertheless fell when the monitors had to withdraw to Dunkirk for re-ammunition. They had indeed used every shell they had. As they withdrew, destroyers dashed as close as they could get to the shore and used their 4 inch armament to maintain the critical barrage. The monitors were back on the 22nd reinforced by some ancient cruisers and gunboats and by the pre-dreadnought battleship *Venerable*. *Venerable* was Admiral Hood's flagship. She drew 25 feet of water and could not operate close inshore, to make use of her 12 inch guns she had to be heeled over so as to extend their range. Her fire was much less effective than the monitor's. This time the bombarding force had to contend with bad weather, making it almost impossible for the monitors to maintain station, they were constantly being blown sideways towards the coastal sandbanks. They had to cease fire at one point as they were rolling so badly that accurate shooting was impossible. There were other interruptions when the guns became too hot to fire, however the bombardment continued until 31 October.

Eventually the front stabilised just east of Nieuwport, and the Belgians opened the flood gates to flood the low lying land around the Yesr river so the enemy could advance no further. It had been a close-run thing, and both sides agreed later that the naval gunfire had turned the tide of the battle. The 6 inch guns had a range of 14,000 yards, enough to outrange enemy field artillery and reach over 2 miles inshore from their firing position 10,000 yards from the coast. This had been just enough to enable the Belgians to establish the defensive line which was to last almost the entire duration of the war. The monitors had received only minor damage during the intense fighting, but had sustained several casualties, including most of the unfortunate machine gun parties which had been landed on the 20th. The importance of this action should not be underestimated. Had the left flank of the Allied armies not held there was little to stop the German armies from occupying Dunkirk, only about 20 miles to the west, and Calais, 25 miles further on. Had they done so the whole strategic situation would have changed and the outcome of the war might well have been different. When the line had stabilised, naval action had to be broken off as heavy long-range guns were being brought up on shore and U-boats were starting to operate out of Zeebrugge. The bombardment would be resumed a few months later as we shall see in a subsequent chapter.

Firing so many rounds at maximum elevation had placed a considerable strain on the Vickers 6 inch guns. High elevation long-range bombardment resulted in increased pressure in the barrels and chambers leading to wear and reduced performance of the gun. As the little ships were urgently required for further service, replacement weapons had to be scavenged from any available source. *Severn* and *Mersey* had their twin 6 inch gun turrets removed entirely and replaced with two old single gun turrets of the same calibre, one forward and one aft. The 4.7 inch howitzers were moved to make room for the new aft turret and mounted up on the boat deck. *Humber*'s guns were in better condition and were retained, and at the same time a third 6 inch gun in a single turret was mounted on her after deck, making her the most heavily armed of the little ships.

Erskine Childers' book '*The Riddle of the Sands*' had had an extraordinary effect on the British public and indeed on military thinking. Throughout the war there were scares that the Germans were about to carry out a landing, using shallow draft barges, on the coast of the east of England, as had been envisaged in Childers' thrilling novel. In reality the Germans had no such plans and had far too much sense to attempt an amphibious operation when the Royal Navy dominated the North Sea. An invasion scare however erupted in November 1914 centred on an imaginary threat of a landing on the muddy shores of the Wash. To deter this, the monitors were sent to spend a chilly winter in Boston, Lincolnshire looking out for non-existent fleets of tugs and barges. They did have some near scrapes with the weather that winter however. At one point they were nearly wrecked off Yarmouth in a northerly gale. They had to leave their anchorage through a shallow unmarked channel as the main entrance would have entailed an easterly heading, bringing the wind on the beam, which would have caused the ungainly craft to roll and skid sideways so much that they would have certainly been wrecked. On another occasion, crossing the Thames Estuary, the wind had shifted to the east and they found that they were making 55 degrees of leeway! A table was drawn up to help navigational calculations:

Wind Force	mph	Leeway
2	13	11.25 deg.
4	23	22.5 deg.
5	28	33.75 deg.
6	34	45 deg.

In anything more than force six, give up.

In early spring they were sent to Dunkirk with the idea of resuming the bombardment, but the weather was too rough and they remained in harbour. Returning to England, there was another unfortunate problem with the weather. A heavy northerly gale and rough sea made *Mersey* totally uncontrollable. She turned her bow stubbornly south and blew towards the French cliffs, whatever the crew did to try to turn her into wind. At the last minute Commander Wilson decided to try to rig a sail aft. Desperately men worked with heavy canvass awnings, and at last a sort of mizzen was hoisted. It did the trick, holding her head to wind, and she staggered home safely.

Early in March a very different role was assigned to the three odd little ships. The Dardanelles campaign was under way and the ever optimistic Churchill was pressing for ships which could support the army on its march up the Danube into the heart of the Austro-Hungarian Empire. These three monitors fitted the bill exactly and they were fitted out for towing to Malta. To prepare them for the hazardous sea passage the ships were strengthened and completely boarded over, the crews being accommodated on a requisitioned civilian liner, *Trent*, where the officers enjoyed the luxury of first class staterooms. Two tugs were allocated to each monitor and off they set at a leisurely 6.5 knots, arriving safely on 29 March. Bad weather prevented them from leaving the island in time to take part in the landings on the Gallipoli peninsular on 25 April, and the monitors remained inactive for a time in the Lazaretto Creek, then they were faced with a sudden change of plan.

The Germans had started the war with a number of commerce raiding cruisers in place on the main trade routes ready to harass British and French civilian shipping. On the whole this was a rather unsuccessful operation as the cruisers faced insuperable difficulties getting coal and were mostly rapidly rounded up by the Royal Navy. One ship, however, *Konigsberg*, (Captain Max Looff) was proving elusive. She was a 3,400 ton light cruiser armed with ten 4.1 inch guns. At the outbreak of the war she sank the British steamer *City of Winchester*, near the mouth of the Red Sea, then cruised south towards Madagascar. Finding no prey there she returned north towards the German East African colonies. En route she came upon HMS *Pegasus*, anchored off Zanzibar, engaged in cleaning her boilers and general maintenance. *Pegasus* was a protected cruiser, built in the 1890s and totally obsolete by 1914. She could make no reply to a sudden assault from the *Konigsberg* and sank with serious loss of life. This was a severe blow to the pride of the Royal Navy and swift revenge was demanded.

Konigsberg had little hope of evading the pack of British cruisers searching for her and retreated into the mouth of the Rufigi river, about 100 miles south of Zanzibar in what was then German East Africa (now part of Tanzania). The River delta is said to be the largest mangrove swamp in the world. *Konigsberg* was soon located by British cruisers and blockaded in the river, but she worked her way upstream, forcing a passage through the mud on a high spring tide, and eventually mooring in a small creek. Here she was located, about 12 miles inland, by a Royal Naval Air Service seaplane. Attempts were made to bombard her, even employing the old battleship *Goliath,* but she was out of effective range from the sea, and the river mouth was too shallow to allow British cruisers to enter (see map 2). The navy could not allow the stalemate to continue. Although *Konigsberg* was harmless in the river, it was impossible to keep a force of cruisers watching the river mouth forever and if the blockade was relaxed she might sneak out and attack the trade routes again. Even if she did not attempt this, it was clear that Allied forces would have to drive the Germans out of East Africa at some point, and her guns could readily be dismounted and used against invading forces. The obvious answer was an attack by the 6 inch shallow draft river monitors.

On 28 April *Severn* and *Mersey* set out for East Africa, again towed by their faithful tugs, still battened down, accompanied by *Trent* and the collier *Kendal Castle*, leaving *Humber*, now the odd man out with her original twin turret, at Malta. The eastern side of the Suez Canal was still in Turkish hands and as they passed through it snipers opened fire on the tugs. Luckily they had been fitted with armoured bridges and sand bagged so no damage was done. There were some scary moments in the Red Sea when a German cruiser was thought to be in the area, luckily this was a false alarm because the convoy would have been easy meat for even a small enemy warship. A more immediate concern was for the safety of the stokers toiling in the engine rooms of the tugs. The daytime temperature was over 100 degrees outside and reached 145 degrees in the engine rooms. Two men died of heat exhaustion and many more were severely affected.

Once past Aden the little convoy encountered headwinds and a strong adverse current, running in places at 5 knots. Progress was slowed to almost zero and something had to be done. Fullerton (now promoted captain) of *Severn*, in command of the force, adopted a novel strategy. *Trent* took *Mersey* in tow and *Kendal Castle* plus three tugs pulled *Severn*, the fourth tug standing by for emergencies. This more than doubled the rate of progress. Off the east African coast there were more problems. Both monitors started to leak seriously and had to be bailed out by men sent aboard with buckets. *Mersey* and one of the tugs went aground and had to be pulled off only moments before their backs would have been broken as they were pounded by the heavy swell as the tide ebbed.

On 3 June they arrived at Mafia Island, at the mouth of the river, which had been recently captured from the Germans. Here they were able to join the blockading squadron. Critically some RNAS aircraft were available, the initial batch of planes had proved unable to operate in tropical conditions but they had rapidly been replaced by newly arrived Henri Farmans and Short seaplanes. These new machines were able to play a vital part in the fighting to come. The banks of the river were thickly forested and strongly occupied by German troops and their native allies and were fortified by some light artillery and machine guns. There were also reports of mines being laid in the river and of onshore torpedo stations. To bring down effective fire on the *Konigsberg* the monitors would have to work their way several miles up the river past these hazards then stop and engage the enemy using aircraft to spot the fall of shot.

No effort was spared to give the ships adequate protection. Extra armour was added above and below the waterlines and the gun turrets were protected by sandbags. Every available empty space below decks was filled with empty petrol tins so as to give buoyancy if they were holed by mines or torpedoes. There was also a vital few days set aside for training. The gunnery officers had to learn rapidly how to work with the RNAS spotters and develop ways of signalling using primitive radio sets and visual signals so as to adjust their aim. This was no easy task given the unreliability of the airborne radio and the time needed to decode signals and pass them to the fire control officers. In practice, rate of fire had to be limited to a maximum of one salvo per minute to give time for signals from the aircraft to be passed and acted on.

At last all was ready and on 6 July the two small monitors left their moorings at 3.30 AM and made use of the darkness to enter the river mouth, guided by flares on ship's boats moored so as to mark the deepest channel. Just before sunrise *Severn*, the leading ship, came under fire from field guns hidden onshore and from small arms (see chart 2). She replied, using her machine guns and 4.7 inch howitzers and soon both ships were steaming up river blazing away at anything which moved onshore and sinking a few native dhows. At one point an attempt was made to launch a torpedo from the shore towards the monitors, but the launch site was seen and destroyed just in time by one of the ship's howitzers. At the same time the blockading cruisers outside the river mouth opened up on the mangrove swamps inland to attempt to confuse the enemy. By 6.30 AM the monitors reached their pre-arranged firing positions about 5 miles downstream from their quarry, anchored fore and aft and made ready to open fire with their 6 inch main armament. By this time fire from the shore was becoming more accurate, making men working the anchors and the guns duck down for cover behind sand bags whenever they could. There was quite a lot of work to do on deck, heaving in and paying out warps, as both anchors were needed to hold the ships across the current so that both their fore and aft turrets could bear on *Konigsberg*. The length of the cables needed constant adjustment. Just before the monitors were ready *Konigsberg* opened up with her main armament, her fire directed by well placed spotters on shore. Both monitors were straddled several times and thousands of dead fish, killed by the exploding shells, floated up to the surface of the river. *Konigsberg* drew first blood, hitting *Mersey*'s fore turret, killing most of the gun crew and putting the turret out of action. She moved a little downriver but continued to fire with her after gun. All the time an aeroplane was spotting the shell bursts of the monitors, but as it was difficult to know which shell came from which monitor and because many shells fell into the mud without exploding, corrections given were often confusing. Also the radio link between the aircraft and the ships was slow and unreliable and air spotting was frequently interrupted when aircraft had to return to Mafia Island to re-fuel. *Severn* eventually scored three hits, none of them lethal, but the enemy's fire began to slacken and the monitors shifted position from time to time making it more difficult for *Konigsberg* to hit them. By mid-afternoon the falling tide forced the monitors to disengage, *Severn* went aground in the process but managed to get off astern. The British had fired 633 rounds of 6 inch during the engagement, but most of these had either not been spotted or failed to explode as they landed in mangrove or mud. The outcome of the day's work was a stalemate, neither side suffering serious damage, but the British had proved to themselves that they could reach their objective and had learnt some vital lessons about how to conduct indirect firing in co-operation with aircraft.

On the 11 July they tried again. There was the usual in-effective bombardment from the shore, but the monitors pressed on towards their previous firing position. This time they split up, *Mersey* anchoring as before with the intention of drawing the enemy fire, while *Severn* pressed on up river sounding the depths constantly, as the charts supplied were extremely inaccurate. The tactic was to enable her to fire on the enemy undisturbed while her sister ship drew the enemy's attention. *Konigsberg* fired one salvo at *Mersey*, which missed, then the German observers on shore realised that *Severn* was the real threat and directed the cruiser's fire onto her. For seventeen uncomfortable minutes, as *Severn* was trying to anchor and warp herself into a good firing posi-tion, salvos rained down on her. Just as the after gun was being brought to bear, four shells landed, two on each side of the after deck and only 3 feet from the ship. Everyone was drenched and splinters whizzed about the deck, but luckily no one was hurt. These well directed shots were made possible partly by aiming marks which had been set up on shore by the Germans on the previous day and partly because one of *Konigsberg*'s officers had concealed himself in a barrel in the mud only a few yards from *Severn*'s position, with a telephone link back to his ship. Unfortunately for him, one of *Severn*'s first salvos happened to sever his telephone line. Soon the spotting aeroplane was in position and firing could commence. *Severn*'s first four salvos disappeared into the mud without exploding, then the range was steadily reduced until bursts were reported 200 yards over and 200 yards to the right. The next was 150 yards short and 100 left. The seventh was lucky, scoring one hit and one very close, eight out of the next twelve shots hit, all on the forepart of *Konigsberg*, putting one of her guns out of action, the aircraft suggested a slight alteration to the left thus putting a second gun out of action. The aeroplane then signalled "I am hit," the seamen saw it glide down with its engine stopped and splash into the river, somersaulting over onto its back. *Mersey*'s motorboat got to the wreck and pulled out two airmen, as one officer put it "uninjured and merry as crickets". They had had a lucky escape, they had been forced to fly quite low – 3,000-4,000 feet because the sky was cloudy; that made them an easy mark for the enemy 12 pounder high angle guns. The plane's engine had started running unevenly and there had been some difficulty in maintaining height, then suddenly there was a terrific bang and a few seconds later the engine stopped altogether. Lieutenant Cull, at the controls did well to come down in the river near the monitors, if he had crashed in the mangroves both he and his observer would certainly have been lost. Whilst aloft they had done a fine job. Signalling the fall of shot from a primitive aircraft under fire, over a hostile jungle, must have been exciting stuff, it is worth remembering that all signalling was by Morse code over an unreliable radio, and the airmen had to watch the fall of shot and signal corrections in less than twenty seconds to give the ship time to adjust her aim for the next salvo. Incredibly, Sub Lieutenant Arnold, the observer, continued to signal the fall of shot even after the aircraft had been hit, thus demonstrating an extraordinarily cool head. The wreck of the Farman could not be salvaged and was blown up with gun cotton.

By now *Severn* had the range of her stationary target. There were several big explosions on *Konigsberg* and her fire from the two remaining guns slackened. *Severn* went on pounding away. Her old guns were starting to get hot and the gunnery control officer had to increase elevation to compensate for the reducing efficiency of the propulsive charges in the hot barrels. *Mersey* then weighed her anchor and steamed on up river cheering *Severn* as she passed her. *Severn* raised her top mast and the captain and some officers climbed to the top to see the damage they had wrought. *Konigsberg* was a smoking wreck, her destruction a testament to the effectiveness of *Severn*'s "second hand" 6 inch guns. *Mersey* then struck the mud a little above *Severn*'s position. This was potentially dangerous as enemy shore based artillery could get close to her and might do damage, however she fired a few rounds at the distant wreck then managed to extricate herself and turned for home. In the end the Germans finished the ruin of their own ship by detonating two torpedo warheads inside her to break her back so that she could not possibly be salvaged. *Severn* finished her day's work by shooting down the telegraph pole which carried the wire from *Konigsberg* to the shore based observers. The monitors steamed proudly back to the river mouth, where tugs were ready to help them across the bar and back to their mooring alongside *Trent*. Admiral King-Hall, in overall command of the operation, steamed past them at high speed in his flagship *Weymouth*, all hands on deck and cheering lustily.

In fact the monitors had had a lucky escape, *Konigsberg* had dispatched two motor boats down a small side creek from which they could emerge downstream of the attackers. Both were armed with torpedoes and these could have proved disastrous for the British. Luckily both boats stuck in the mud and could not get off until just after the monitors had left.

Konigsberg had suffered thirty killed and 125 wounded, the surviving crew marched inland and were incorporated into the local defence force as an infantry battalion. Some days after she had been abandoned a party of divers and engineers was sent to salvage her ten 4.1 inch rapid firing guns, all of which were able to be made serviceable, and other useful components of the ship.

Very important lessons were learnt from this engagement. The first of these was that even with the primitive equipment then available, spotting from the air can work well provided that only one ship is firing at a time. Fire from two or more made it almost impossible. The second was that the monitors, with their low freeboard and minimal upper works, were a very difficult target. At a range of 3-5 miles. They were straddled many times but only hit once. A ship riding higher in the water would probably have suffered serious damage, as the German gunnery was excellent. A third lesson was that a stationary monitor could be expected to hit a stationary target at quite long ranges, even with indirect fire, provided that the spotting was good. Five miles was considered a very long range for a 6 inch gun at the time, and *Severn* was able to hit her opponent quite reliably at this distance, indeed at about 3 miles she was obtaining one hit every 72 seconds. Altogether the action was a vindication of the monitor concept, although it was of only peripheral importance to the course of the war.

German East Africa was still strongly held by the enemy on land, and the monitors, after some repairs at Zanzibar, were retained on the Africa station to try to prevent the colony being re-supplied by sea.

Their next action was against Tanga, a coastal town situated just south of the border between modern Tanzania and Kenya. Tanga had a shallow harbour which connected with a railway running inland. The Royal Navy had the task of making sure this was not used. Early in August intelligence had found out that a modern steamer *Margraf* was in the harbour and that another enemy supply ship was expected to arrive soon. On the 19th the monitors with two armed whale catchers, sprung a surprise attack on the harbour. The idea was that the whale catchers would secure alongside *Margraf* and any other ship in the harbour and either capture or sink her, supported by the guns of the monitors. At dawn they entered the harbour at maximum speed and found, to their surprise, a cable across the entrance. They were able to cross this hazard however, as in places it was 10 feet under water, and they found *Margraf* aground on the other side. The whale boats got alongside, but fire from the shore – some of it probably from the guns salvaged from *Konigsberg* – was so heavy and accurate that they had to withdraw. It was left to the monitors to smash the steamer to pieces with their guns. There were several hits on *Severn* from the shore guns but there was not much damage and only one unfortunate midshipman was wounded. On their way out of the harbour the ships saw the purpose of the cable across the mouth. At the landward end of it was a barge loaded with mines, these would normally have been moored to the cable, but had been removed to allow an incoming ship to enter. The barge made a wonderful target and blew up with a most satisfactory explosion. As they left, the departing monitors engaged and destroyed a fort and tower at the harbour mouth.

The navy had not finished with Tanga. After a period of patrolling the coast, *Severn* together with the old battleship *Vengeance*, made another attack on the harbour and destroyed the railway station. After more alarms and excursions the port was eventually captured. The monitors then moved on to participate in the capture of Dar-es-Salaam and

Bagamoyo, and, again in conjunction with *Vengeance* and some ancient cruisers, drove the enemy from all his coastal positions so that the German colony could not possibly be supplied from the sea. Finally they co-operated with army units moving inland, giving fire support from positions up the shallow, muddy creeks of the local rivers. In May 1918 they returned to the Mediterranean, job well done.

The operations in East Africa had been something of a sideshow in the war, but the little ships had done work which would have been impossible for any other type and had proved themselves astonishingly tough and versatile. Working up muddy creeks and in shallow harbours they had been able to bring their firepower to bear where no other ship could venture and where the enemy least expected it. The Admiralty got astonishingly good value for the £115,000 apiece it had paid for these strange little river craft.

Chapter 4

The Gallipoli Campaign

While the first two monitors were active on the coast of Africa events of far greater importance were taking place in the Dardanelles. It was to prove one of the most disastrous actions ever undertaken by British arms. After Troubridge had been sent home in disgrace for letting *Goeben* escape, Admiral Sir Sackville Carden was placed in command of the force which was to find her, if she dared to emerge from her Turkish lair, and sink her and her consort. His task was not an easy one (see map 3).

The Narrows, the passage leading from the Aegean to the Sea of Marmora was protected by powerful forts on Cape Helles and Kum Kale and by further batteries of heavy guns at Kephez and Chanak points. Even more dangerous than these was a dense minefield consisting of almost 400 moored mines in the channel which was less than 1 mile wide.

A quick look at chart 3 will show the nature of the task which the navy faced. The Straits are dominated by hilly, broken country and are only about 5 miles wide at their widest point. Ships in the Straits are liable to shelling from the forts at the entrance and from others established at strategic points along the shoreline. The forts themselves were venerable structures, but around them had been built, with German advice and help, modern well designed earth-works concealing heavy guns which could survive anything short of a direct hit on the gun itself. In the hillsides looking down on the Straits were concealed mobile batteries of field guns and howitzers. These were not big enough to damage heavily armoured ships much, but they could be fatal to unarmoured vessels such as trawlers or destroyers. There were also powerful mobile searchlights to spot for the guns at night. Through the Straits runs a current of anything from 2 to 4 knots, constantly running out into the Mediterranean. This current runs strongly in the centre, but is weak or non-existent near the shores, especially the southern (Asiatic) shore. There could scarcely be a more suitable stretch of water for defensive mining.

The Narrows of the Dardanelles had been mined before the war, in mid-1914, but merchant ships were allowed to pass through a clear channel, accompanied by a Turkish pilot. In September of that year however a British patrol inter-cepted a Turkish destroyer just outside the Narrows and found German sailors on board. The resulting diplomatic incident caused the Turks to close the gap in the minefields and declare the Narrows closed, cutting Russia off from the Mediterranean. On 31 October Turkey joined the war on the German side. Immediately the minefields were reinforced, and the shore based heavy artillery and mobile field guns were increased in number. Their crews were rapidly stiff-ened by newly arrived German artillery specialists. More powerful searchlights were sent to cover the minefields and keep away sweepers. The old battleship *Messudieh* was sent into the Narrows to provide extra protection and fire power. Carden made two attempts to destroy forts guarding the entrance, doing considerable damage, but failing to silence them completely. The protective earthworks, reinforced with German help, ensured that although the guns might be dismounted and the gunners evacuated during a daylight bombardment, it was a relatively simple matter to restore them during the hours of darkness. Only a direct hit on the gun itself would effectively destroy it. The only notable Allied success was the sinking of *Messudieh* by the submarine *B-11*, which managed to dive below the mines and stem the current in the Narrows, although her underwater speed was only 4 knots.

By the end of January 1915 the War Cabinet had determined to adopt a more aggressive policy with the hope of forcing Turkey out of the war altogether. A fleet of ten British and four French old pre-dreadnought battleships would force the Narrows and steam towards Constantinople, protected by minesweepers and destroyers. The entrance forts would be silenced by their guns, supported by the great 15 inch main armament of *Queen Elizabeth*, the navy's most modern and formidable battleship, which had been sent out by the Admiralty to provide support. She was not allowed to penetrate the Straits themselves – that would be too risky – but she could bombard from far off. Unfortunately accurate long-range indirect gunfire was impossible without good spotting from the air, and this, for various reasons, was not available. Carden had proposed this scheme and it was endorsed by the War Cabinet in the face of opposition from Fisher, the First Sea Lord who correctly foresaw the danger from mines and the problems associated with attacking coastal artillery from the sea.

The attacks on the forts commenced on 19 February, and by 25th most of the guns in the outer forts had been destroyed by the ship's bombardment and by Royal Marine landing parties. The fleets were now able to move into the mouth of the Straits and silence the inner forts guarding the entrance to the Narrows. This was less successful, once again the Turkish gunners took cover when they were being hit by naval gunfire, only to emerge as soon as it ceased, furthermore, as the ships entered the restricted waters, they came within range of the mobile field guns. These could not do severe damage to heavy ships but they did make matters extremely difficult for the intruders, and forced the unarmoured destroyers to keep moving so as to avoid being hit. Firing on the inner forts at long range did little damage to them and it was clear that the warships would have to get closer for their assault to be effective.

The first section of the Strait was clear of mines, but to move further in and tackle the second pair of forts at the entrance to the Narrows themselves at close range, the minefields would have to be swept. To do this, North Sea trawlers had been provided, and these were given light armour to protect them from small arms fire. They were manned by their regular RNMR (Royal Naval Minesweeping Reserve) crews. It had originally been intended to supplement these with "mine bumpers" – cargo ships with reinforced hulls filled with concrete which would clear a path for each capital ship by steaming through the field blowing up mines as they went. These were not eventually provided. (Strangely the British did not make much use of reinforced mine bumpers to protect capital ships in either world war. The Germans used them, calling them Speerbrechers, extensively in both). The trawlers had to battle against the strong currents in the Straits, so that their speed over the land was only 2 or 3 knots making them easy targets for guns on shore. To give them some protection from shore batteries, the sweepers were detailed to work at night and were supported by destroyers and a light cruiser. On 1 March they set off on their first mission. Before they reached the minefield they were detected from the shore, and illuminated by brilliant search-lights, making them an excellent target for the shore based field guns. No trawlers were hit, but the fisherman crews hastily withdrew. They had not been trained for work under fire and were badly shaken by the experience. Who can blame them? Their little ships were almost stationary in the strong current, and a single hit from the 4 inch or 6 inch field guns would have proved fatal. Three more attempts were made, but with no result. A new approach was then tried. This time the trawlers steamed up stream as fast as they could go, with their sweeping gear stowed, then turned and swept down with the current. A handful of mines were recovered, but some of the crews were so scared, especially when they had to turn round and deploy their sweeps under fire, that they did not attempt to sweep at all. After two weeks of failure the regular navy was becoming disillusioned with the fishermen-sweepers. One trawler had been sunk and several damaged, but no one had been killed and there were open accusations of cowardice levelled at the RNMR. On 13 March one final attempt was made with the sweeper crews stiffened with Royal Navy volunteers and supported again by fire from a battleship. This was even more disastrous. The supporting cruiser *Amethyst* was badly hit, suffering twenty-four men killed, and several trawlers were severely damaged, also suffering casualties. A few mines were swept, and some more were found floating free in the Straits. Possibly these had been deliberately floated down by the Turks. They were easily dealt with and in future operations small picket boats operated alongside major ships to deal with any more "floaters". This was a pretty high risk operation for the picket boat's crews, exposed as they were to the fire of field guns on shore. Some of them were actually fitted with explosive sweeping wires and seem to have accounted for several mines.

By this point Carden was coming under severe pressure from Churchill who urged him to make progress regardless of casualties. After all, he argued, thousands were dying on the western front and the Dardanelles operation could relieve pressure on the hard-pressed troops in France. It was well worth hundreds of casualties among the minesweepers to force the passage and achieve their objective. The minesweeper crews, not unnaturally, did not agree.

The unfortunate Carden fell sick and was replaced by Admiral de Robeck, who had been his second in command. He resolved to continue the attack but to use a new tactic, devised by Carden, of making a daylight attack on the shore batteries and to sweep the minefields as he went. He intended to use his full force now consisting of thirteen British and four French battleships, and one dreadnought battle cruiser. The battleships were all pre-dreadnoughts except for the super dreadnought *Queen Elizabeth*, still attempting to make her indirect fire from outside the Narrows effective. A heavy bombardment at long range would attempt to silence the shore batteries and suppress the guns in the forts, then a second wave of battleships would steam close to the forts and complete their destruction, covering the passage of trawlers into the minefields. The warships could then follow the sweepers and force their way right through the Narrows. Some of the attendant destroyers were adapted to carry light sweeping gear.

The action took place on 18 March. At first things went as planned, the armada steamed into the straight and advanced towards the forts on Kephez Point, Turkish shore batteries replied vigorously, but the only ship badly damaged was the French *Gaulois,* which had to be beached. Gradually the warships got the better of the shore guns, and things were going according to plan when the advancing second line of battleships, steaming close to the forts to blast them at close range, suffered a series of appalling disasters. *Bouvet* (French) and *Irresistible* (British) were sunk by mines where there should have been none, and the battle cruiser *Inflexible* was severely damaged by gunfire. Shortly afterwards the battleship *Ocean* was disabled by gunfire and a mine strike and had to be abandoned. Once again, to the disgust of the naval officers present, the trawlers fled from the scene under heavy bombardment. Two of them had tried to deploy their sweeps and steam upstream. They dealt with three moored mines, but fire from the shore was too much for them and they abandoned their attempt in spite of orders and encouragement shouted from the picket boats and destroyers. It was impossible now for the battleships to proceed into the Narrows and de Robeck had no alternative to withdrawing his battered force. What had happened was that a Turkish mine expert, Lieutenant Colonel Geehl, had anticipated a close range attack on the inner forts and had taken the small fast steamer *Nousret* down the Narrows and laid a small field of twenty mines in exactly the right position. Hence an insignificant little civilian craft had brought about the sinking of three major warships and the disablement of a dreadnought battle cruiser. From that day on de Robeck was determined that no further attempt could be made to force a passage into the Sea of Marmora, until at least the European shore was held by the

Allies. The Admiralty supported him and the scene was set for the even greater disaster of the landings on the Gallipoli Peninsula.

This sorry performance made the navy keener than ever on the idea of the monitors. If big gun monitors, such as the 14 inch, 12 inch and 15 inch vessels then being built, had been available to get close to the coastal guns, things might have gone differently, or so it was argued in Whitehall. The monitor's big guns could have been brought to bear on the forts from close range, as they could operate in shallow water, close under the enemy guns, and their mine defences and shallow draft would have at least reduced the possibility of their sharing *Ocean*'s fate. Monitors must be got to the Aegean as quickly as possible.

Humber, it will be recalled, had remained at Malta while her sisters were making their way down the African coast. A small ship with only three 6 inch guns and two howitzers she seems to have been overlooked, in any case her mission had been to act as a river craft when the march up the Danube began. Then the great events taking place at Gallipoli brought a sudden change.

General, Sir Ian Hamilton, who had arrived just in time to witness the events of the 18 March, and was to command military operations on land, had agreed with de Robeck that the army would have to occupy the northern shore and destroy the enemy forts once and for all before any further naval assault on the Narrows could be contemplated. Churchill, as First Lord of the Admiralty objected strongly to this scheme and ordered de Robeck to resume his naval offensive but the order was countermanded at the insistence of Fisher. 75,000 troops had been earmarked for landing at Gallipoli, consisting of Australians and New Zealanders then training in Egypt, the British 29th Division and a French North African Division. Hamilton had been assured that his task would be easy. The whole peninsular would be swept by naval gunfire, the Turks would put up only a token resistance as the bulk of their troops would be busy elsewhere and the affair would be over in a few weeks. It appears that no one had taken the trouble to find out that the ground on which the army would be fighting was rugged and desolate, rising in places to 1,000 feet in height and ideal for defensive warfare. The Turkish army was indeed ill equipped and poorly trained, but it was stiffened by highly professional German officers and supplied with some excellent German weapons, especially machine guns and artillery. In command was the redoubtable General Otto von Sanders.

The Allied army took some time to organise itself, giving von Sanders the opportunity to make an excellent job of fortifying the peninsular. The landings took place on 25 April, gradually and with terrible losses, the troops battled their way inland constantly supported by the guns of the fleet. It soon became clear, however, that naval support, critical as it was to the campaign, could not be maintained. For the first month all went well for the fleet, although their bombardment of the enemy positions ashore was not nearly as effective as everyone had hoped, due to the rugged terrain and the excellent defences built by the Turks. Commodore Roger Keyes, Chief of Staff to de Robeck, who was the strongest advocate of a further attempt to force the Narrows by the now much increased Allied fleet, confessed to being ashamed of the relative inactivity of the navy while so many soldiers were dying ashore. Then, on the 12 May the battleship *Goliath*, lying just 100 yards off-shore and waiting to be allocated a new target, noticed an unfamiliar looking destroyer approaching her during the night. The officer of the watch challenged the stranger, but he was too late. The ship was the Turkish destroyer *Muavenet,* her German captain had skilfully brought her down the Narrows, close inshore on the European side and she let loose three torpedoes at close range. *Goliath* rolled over and turned turtle, rapidly sinking. There was a strong current running at an estimated 4-5 knots so men attempting to swim ashore were all carried away and drowned. Out of 750 men on board only 180 were saved by boats from nearby ships. This disaster set off an almighty row in the Admiralty. Fisher, who had always disliked the whole idea of the Dardanelles campaign, was in a fever of worry about the possibility of *Queen Elizabeth,* the super dread-nought, suffering the same fate. Churchill pacified him by agreeing to withdraw *Queen Elizabeth* and replace her as soon as possible with 14 inch monitors. This was set in hand, but as soon as the War Office heard of it Lord Kitchener objected violently. "If she goes," he said, "we may have to consider . . . whether the troops had better be pulled back to Alexandria". The navy, it seemed to him, was deserting the army in its hour of need. Fisher was adamant and stated that if *Queen Elizabeth* did not sail that very night he himself would walk out of the Admiralty. Tempers were temporarily cooled by the promise of sending still more monitors and bringing home some more battleships, but this had the effect of annoying Fisher again as he had hoped to use the monitors for his scheme for a landing on Germany's Baltic coast. He resigned in a fury and played no further part in the war.

The navy's problems were only just beginning however, on 17 May *U.21* had been sighted passing through the Straits of Gibraltar. Admiral de Robeck was informed but seems to have taken no new precautions. On 25th the old battleship

Triumph was standing off Anzac Beach in full view of both armies. She suddenly rolled over and sank, a victim of the first of *U.21's* torpedoes. The Turks in their trenches shouted and danced for joy as she went down, mercifully with the loss of only fifty-six men. The following day *Majestic*, another ancient battleship, was preparing to fire on the Turkish trenches when a seaman said to an officer "Look Sir, there is a submarine's conning tower." "Yes" he replied, "and here comes the torpedo." The old battleship rolled over and lay in the shallow water, her hull just awash. The Allies had clearly lost control of the waters close to the peninsula. The following day a German officer, looking down from the heights, was astonished to see the water which had once been alive with British warships almost deserted. The fleet had retired to safe anchorages around Murdros Island leaving the hard pressed troops ashore almost without heavy gun support. It was whispered in the trenches that the navy had run away.

Then someone remembered *Humber*. She was at Malta, she was expendable, there didn't seem to be much prospect of sending her up the Danube and if she could replace the heavy warships withdrawn she would at least be better than nothing. At the same time some cruisers, hastily fitted with anti-torpedo bulges, were pressed into the bombardment squadron and sent to cruise off the peninsula. On 4 June *Humber* started to bombard an especially troublesome nest of Turkish artillery hidden among the olive trees in a ravine called Axmah. Her intervention was most welcome to the beleaguered troops on shore and she was able to provide effective bombardment with her 6 inch guns and also use the two 4.5 inch howitzers for high trajectory fire into ravines and trenches. There was a problem the following day when a premature detonation damaged one of her forward guns, but she remained in action until December, becoming a bit of a favourite with the Anzac troops, who were short of artillery of their own. They were constantly pestered by Turkish guns hidden in olive groves which enfiladed the beaches over which all their reinforcements and supplies had to travel. Working very close to the shore *Humber* was often fired on by enemy field guns, but never seriously damaged. After the loss of the three battleships, the bombardment squadrons of monitors and cruisers were careful to deploy their torpedo nets and were not troubled by enemy submarines or destroyers. They put up an impressive performance.

The bitter rows in London about the deployment of *Queen Elizabeth,* and the possibility of attacks on the German coast had resulted in the dispatch of the first of the specially built 14 inch monitors, the four "Generals" with the American built 14 inch guns, to join the makeshift fleet supporting the Dardanelles operation. Their departure was delayed by the need to replace the wrongly designed propellers and correct other faults found on trials. They were so slow and under-powered that they had to be towed for most of the 3,000 mile voyage. *Abercrombie,* towed by the old cruiser *Thesus* set off on 24 June, *Havelock, Raglan* and *Roberts* leaving a few days later also under tow. They arrived at Murdros in late July, and the sight of their massive turrets must have put new heart into troops on shore.

As soon as she arrived *Abercrombie* targeted ammunition dumps on shore at Eren Keui on the Asiatic shore, the Turks replied and she was hit by a heavy shell which luckily did not explode. Her own fire seems to have been ineffective, possibly because of lack of proper spotting from aircraft. It had always been intended that large monitors should carry their own spotter planes, but these were found to be a nuisance because they were a fire hazard, and because they had to be removed every time the guns were fired as the shock damaged them. *Roberts* joined *Abercrombie* in mid-July and she was tasked to destroy heavy gun batteries on the Asiatic shore, near Kum Kale, which were able to fire on the flank of the troops trying to force their way forward up the Cape Helles peninsula. To do this she anchored off Rabbit Island. This was to be a favourite berth for monitors for many months, it was over 10 miles from their target, well within range of the 14 inch guns but hidden behind the island and far enough away from the enemy to be almost immune from counter fire. The monitor's own fire was indirect, they could not see their targets, but aiming marks on the island enabled the guns to be correctly aligned. The Turkish batteries were never totally destroyed, but their fire was much reduced. Occasionally aircraft attempted to bomb the monitors but they did little damage.

On 6 and 7 August the Allies landed reinforcements at Sulva Bay, this action was supported by the final two 14 inch monitors, *Havelock* and *Raglan* and by some of the small monitors which had now arrived on the scene straight from their builders. Once again the main targets were mobile Turkish batteries and troop concentrations. Naval support was critical to the success of the landing, although on one occasion a naval gun, firing prematurely, landed a shell among British troops causing four casualties. *Havelock* moved into Sulva Bay itself, giving direct close fire support to troops, but it soon became clear that ammunition ex-penditure was becoming excessive and had to be curtailed. It seems that the process of spotting and communication between the ships and observers on land and in the air during these operations left something to be desired. The lessons being learnt at almost the same time by *Severn* and *Mersey* about developing very close relations between the airmen and the gun crews, working out easily understood codes and keeping the spotter's job as simple as possible, were not so easy to apply in the complicated situation of the Gallipoli campaign. Frequently the monitors operated very close to the shore in support of ground forces, and were in range of Turkish guns. Most of these were 75mm (approximately 12lb.) which could do little damage to the ships. Splinters could of course kill crewmen in the open, but only on rare occasions was anyone needed on deck during firing operations. There were some bigger guns as well, but Turkish shooting was not the best and no serious damage was done. Occasionally very long range bombardment was called for, and for this the ships would be heeled over by flooding the anti-torpedo bulges so as to give extra elevation. This put extra strain on the guns and turrets reducing the life of the gun barrels, so the technique had to be used sparingly.

As 1915 progressed stalemate developed on the peninsula. The Sulva landings had broadened the Allied front but had been contained by the Turks, who held firm on the high ground. Also the 14 inch monitors were starting to show some weaknesses, especially in their steering engines and, in some cases, in their much abused gun barrels. A repair ship, *Reliance*, was at Murdros and worked hard to keep them in action. It was obvious that the monitors would never be able to force a passage up the Narrows as they could barely stem the current. In the autumn, as more of the small monitors appeared on the scene, a re-organisation of naval forces was undertaken and four bombardment divisions were formed comprising:

The four 14 inch monitors.

Ten 9.2 inch small monitors *M15-M23 + M28*.

Five 6 inch monitors *M29-M33 + Humber*.

Four bulged cruisers.

Gradually, with experience, the fire of the big monitors became more effective. *Roberts* remained off Rabbit Island, *Abercrombie* supported the left flank of the Cape Helles beachhead, firing on batteries on the slopes of Achi Baba. Her accurate and effective fire drew heartening compliments from senior army officers. *Havelock* seems to have specialised in long range bombardment, firing right over the peninsula, on one occasion hitting an armaments dump 17,000 yards away eleven times out of fifteen shots. *Raglan* continued to support the Sulva Bay position then moved off on another mission.

Serbia was being threatened by Bulgaria and an Allied contingent was landed to support the Serbs. A small naval squadron was dispatched to the Aegean in support, *Raglan*'s heavy guns were considered a useful addition to the cruisers and destroyers involved, but in the end there was very little fighting (see map 4).

Although it became plain to most observers by the end of the summer of 1915 that the land battle at Gallipoli was making no progress, the momentum of the campaign caused it to drag on until December and more and more monitors of various kinds started to appear as the campaign progressed. The small monitors being faster and handier than the heavy gun ships were particularly effective at harassing the coastline of European Turkey. The 9.2 inch guns, old as they were, proved to be most accurate and effective weapons, although their recoil was such that the little ships lurched violently each time they were fired. They were invaluable in suppressing enemy counter fire aimed at their big sisters and in firing at long range at enemy ships in the Narrows. Their 9.2 and 6 inch ammunition was not in such short supply as 14 inch so they could be more liberally used. One exciting side show action was carried out against Bulgaria during October when the 9.2's of *M15*, *M19* and *M28* bombarded Bulgarian railway installations and barracks at Dedeagatch (see map 4). Much damage was done and the Bulgarians, fearing an Allied invasion, were forced to adopt a defensive posture in place of supporting their allies against Serbia.

In spite of their relative simplicity the small monitors did present some problems for the fleet's engineers. The diesel engine ships often suffered funnel fires due to hot exhaust gasses setting fire to soot deposits in the funnels, although the results of these could be alarming they were seldom serious. *M19* suffered a more serious problem when she was moored alongside *Abercrombie* and joining in a bombardment of the slopes on Achi Baba. Suddenly she appeared to be in the middle of a colossal explosion and chunks of metal rained down all round her. What had happened was that a shell had exploded inside the bore of her gun blowing it to pieces and setting fire to the magazine. Acting promptly and coolly the crew flooded the magazine and got the fire under control. Two men had been killed and another injured by a fragment which came in through the slits in the armoured conning tower, six others suffered serious burns. The ship managed to limp to Malta where she was repaired. Another casualty was *M30*, patrolling off Smyrna (Izmura) in Asiatic Turkey.

She was hit by a well concealed heavy gun onshore and caught fire. This time the fire spread to the fuel and she had to be abandoned. Her guns were eventually recovered and the hull was blown up.

In December the eventual abandonment of the Dardanelles commenced and it was completed by the 8 January. The withdrawal had become strategically inevitable. The army was making almost no progress on land, and losses were mounting steadily, not just from enemy action, but from the bitter cold and freezing rain storms which started in October and grew steadily worse. Bulgaria's entry into the war meant that there was even less prospect than before of a thrust up the Danube to attack the flank of the Austrian army. Hamilton, who had gloomily forecast that half his men would be lost if the force was evacuated, was relieved of his command. His replacement, General, Sir Charles Monro, arrived fresh from the western front, made no secret of his belief that the whole Gallipoli affair was a waste of time and of resources desperately needed elsewhere. Commodore Roger Keyes still believed that a last attempt to force the Narrows should be made by the fleet reinforced by fast minesweepers, but now that Arthur Balfour had taken over the Admiralty from Churchill, and de Roebeck remained staunchly opposed to any such venture, Keyes's appeals fell on deaf ears.

In sharp contrast to most of the campaign, the evacuation was brilliantly handled with rifles and artillery arranged to continue firing after the troops had withdrawn so as to disguise the fact that the withdrawal was taking place. Almost all the monitors, including two of the new 12 inch ships which had just arrived from Britain, together with the bulged cruisers, had been assembled to cover the final evacuation from the beaches and the whole operation was completed without a hitch and with minimal casualties. Of the half a million men involved in the Gallipoli expedition almost half had been wounded or became sick, 50,000 died.

This ill-conceived campaign had shown up very well the strengths and weaknesses of the big gun monitors. They had provided useful fire cover and destroyed some important enemy installations but their interventions had not been in any way decisive and their co-ordination with ground forces had not always been good. They were so slow that they were utterly useless for the operation which it had been hoped they could perform – forcing the Narrows. Furthermore their appetite for heavy ammunition was a serious embarrassment on this station, distant as it was from Great Britain. For most of the campaign the 14 inch monitors had to be limited to two or three rounds per day. Land battles in the 1914-1918 war were won by using massed artillery pouring thousands of rounds down in a hail of fire on enemy positions, and this could not be achieved using the great guns of the monitors on this distant battlefield. Introduced as a cheap, quickly constructed force which would allow Britain to project military might overseas and carry the battle to the enemy, these limitations of the monitors must have been a sore disappointment to everyone involved. Conversely the small monitors had been reasonably successful. Their guns had been effective, especially the old 9.2s and because they were small and readily mobile they had done everything that could be expected of them, effectively harassing enemy lines of communication and making movement by land or water along the coastline extremely difficult. They were also useful for patrolling the narrow seas between Greece and Turkey, keeping a lookout for suspicious movements, a task for which they were to be used extensively in later campaigns.

After the evacuation of the peninsular, six large monitors remained in the eastern Mediterranean. These were *Abercrombie, Raglan, Havelock* and *Roberts* (14 inch), *Picton* and *Peterborough* (12 inch), together with their 9.2 inch and 6 inch sisters. *Havelock* and *Roberts* were sent home and spent the rest of the war doing the intensely boring jobs of acting as guard ships for Yarmouth and Lowestoft. There were still a number of duties in the Middle East to be performed however for which the remaining ships would be suitable.

Abercrombie remained off the Dardanelles, occasionally bombarding enemy ships in the Narrows and any targets of opportunity which might emerge on land. The only serious opposition she suffered was from enemy aircraft, who would come over and bomb or machine gun her from time to time. The art of anti-aircraft fire was in its infancy but luckily so was the science of high level bombing, so little damage was done. The worst incident occurred when she managed to fire her own high angle 3 pounder gun into a pile of petrol cans on deck creating a spectacular fire. Luckily the only damage was to a canteen store which was flooded as a fire precaution. Her other duty on this station was to look out for the dreaded *Goeben,* still lurking somewhere to the east. This work was alternated with patrols off the Turkish coast around Smyrna and further north in the Aegean. This was not a very active theatre, although she was once unsuccessfully attacked by a submarine. On another occasion she made an attack on railway facilities in Bulgaria, close to those targeted by the small monitors in 1915. Here her shooting was particularly good and much damage was done.

Raglan had a more exciting time. Like her sister she

patrolled off Smyrna and in the Aegean, occasionally finding a worthwhile target. Next, in October 1917, she was employed together with four small monitors to support the General Allenby's advance into Gaza and Palestine. The idea was to use naval forces to create a diversion on the coast while the army moved up further inland. The exercise was carried out with some success making use of spotter planes from the seaplane carrier, *City of Oxford*. This operation continued for a week doing great damage to enemy supplies and communications. The bombardment concluded when the fighting moved further inland, out of range of naval guns. The monitors were still in the area when reports of a lurking U-boat sent the warships to shelter behind nets in a prepared anchorage. *UC.38* however slipped round the end of the nets, unseen by the patrolling trawlers, and put torpedoes into *M15* and the destroyer *Staunch*. *M15* caught fire and sank with the loss of twenty-six men. The remaining monitors then moved north again up the coast and shelled the routed Turkish Army as it retreated north of Jaffa.

This operation complete, *Raglan* plodded back to Rabbit Island and the *Goeben* watch. Here she was threatened by some newly mounted heavy guns on Cape Helles which she soon engaged in company with some of the small monitors. As usual the guns were silenced for a time, but soon recovered and were never totally destroyed. The little squadron then moved north and shot up Bulgarian shore installations east of Stavros. *Raglan's* next stopping place was Imbros Island, right at the entrance of the Dardanelles where she anchored on 26 December 1917, in Kusu Bay, 15 miles from the entrance to the straights, in company with the 9.2 inch small monitor *M28* (see map 4). This anchorage had the advantage of being out of range of the guns on Cape Helles.

There had been some vague rumours that *Goeben* might be planning a sortie, but the waters around the entrance to the Dardanelles had been extensively mined so it seemed probable that any movement by the battle cruiser would be heralded by a mine sweeping operation so no special precautions were taken. Since their dramatic dash to Constantinople, *Goeben* and *Breslau* had made some ventures into the Black Sea and been engaged in a number of actions with the Russian fleet. *Goeben* had suffered some damage from mines and had been temporally patched up with concrete as there was no dry dock in Turkey where she could make a proper repair. Lack of proper facilities had taken their toll in other ways, so her speed was reduced but her armament was still in good condition.

Besides the two monitors, the *Goeben* watch consisted of two old battleships based at Mudros, 20 miles to the south west and some supporting cruisers and destroyers. There was also a lookout post at Mavro, on Rabbit Island, close to the mouth of the Straight.

On a misty Sunday morning on 20 January 1918, the two enemy ships did indeed steam down the Narrows, without waiting for minesweepers, and slipped past Mavro unseen in the hazy morning light. They held a westerly course, towards Mudros, at first skirting the British minefield. They were aware of its existence but not of its full extent. After thirty minutes *Goeben* struck an outlying mine, but German ships were extremely well designed to survive mine strikes and on this occasion the damage was not serious, so it was decided to continue the sortie. At about 7 AM the two ships looked into Aliki Bay, frequently used as an anchorage by the British, but on this occasion it was empty. Thinking that the watching squadron must be somewhere on the east coast of Imbros they steamed close inshore, taking the occasion to bombard a signal station at Kephalo. At 7.20 AM they were sighted by the destroyer *Lizard* which was on patrol near the north east tip of Imbros. *Lizard* immediately realised the danger faced by the two monitors, which were anchored and going about their Sunday morning routines in Kusu bay, a few miles to the north, she tried frantically to contact them by radio, but the Germans were jamming her signals and it took ten minutes to get through. At almost the moment she received *Lizard*'s signal, *Raglan* sighted the enemy and action stations was sounded. At the same time a signal was sent to the battleships at Mudros. The monitors were camouflaged and hoped that they had not been spotted against the shore as they traversed their guns towards the enemy. Hopes were soon dashed. *Breslau,* in the lead, opened fire on *Lizard* to prevent her from making a torpedo attack, then turned her 5.9 inch guns on *Raglan*. Her first salvo was 1,000 yards short and *Raglan* was able to reply using her 6 inch turret in local control while the 14 inch was being made ready. *Raglan*'s first round missed and *Breslau*'s second shot was closer, about 500 yards short. *Raglan*'s 14 inch was now brought into play, but its first round fell astern of the attacker and *Breslau*'s third salvo was just over, her stationary target had thus been bracketed in a classic exercise of the art of naval gunnery. Her next round smashed into *Raglan*'s fire control tower. This was extremely serious as it made accurate shooting very difficult, and *Breslau* was able to send salvo after salvo into the hull of the monitor, damaging the engine room, cutting off power supplies and eventually interrupting the ammunition supply to the 6 inch gun. This had been firing to some effect and may have achieved two hits, one on *Breslau* and one on *Goeben*. *Goeben* herself had now emerged round the headland and almost immediately achieved a hit on *Raglan*'s main turret with her 11 inch main armament. This penetrated the armour, killed several people and set off secondary explosions. The order was given to abandon ship, and survivors swam the short distance to the shore. *Breslau* now turned her fire on *M28*. Her second salvo hit amidships setting fire to her cordite and fuel oil so rendering her helpless. Attempts by trawlers to lay a smokescreen to protect the monitors had failed and now they were both helpless wrecks. The Germans were able to finish them off at a range of only 4,000 yards. By coincidence a whaler from *M28,* which had been picking up survivors from *Raglan* as she sank with her mast still showing above water, returned to its mother ship at the very moment when *M28*'s own magazine blew up. The men in the little whaler were deafened but had a lucky escape.

This had been a daring and skilful action by the German Imperial Navy, who displayed typical skill and fighting spirit. As ever their gunnery had been excellent, quickly finding the range and doing terrible damage before their opponents could reply. *Breslau*'s action was especially distinguished, she went straight for two ships, both with much heavier guns than her own, while at the same time fending off a destroyer attack. Unfortunately for her this was not the end of the story.

The two German ships now turned south again, aiming to follow their previous track then turned westward so as to try to repeat their success by catching the battleships off guard at Mudros. This time however they strayed a little further from the island shore and found themselves in the minefield. By 9.05 AM *Breslau* had struck at least six mines and was also under attack from aircraft. She sank rapidly. *Goeben* struck two more mines and was now seriously damaged, but she could still make way, and successfully fought off an attack by the destroyers *Lizard* and *Tigress*. She limped back to the relative safety of the Dardanelles where she beached herself. Admiral Hayes-Sadler, who was in command of the squadron at Murdros, asked the Admiralty to send him a 15 inch monitor to finish *Goeben* off from outside the strait, but this was obviously impractical at short notice. Instead *M17* was called on and she anchored off the peninsula on 24 January and opened fire. Unfortunately the weather was hazy so spotting was difficult and no hits seem to have been made. Eventually she had to withdraw on account of bombardment from the shore. It is most surprising that *Abercrombie*, which was in Mudros at the time was not used for this duty. She would have been better able to absorb the counter fire and her 14 inch main armament would certainly have been more damaging than *M17*'s 9.5s. *Goeben* was eventually patched and towed off the sandbank by a Turkish pre-dreadnought battleship. She was now effectively disabled for the rest of the war.

One hundred and twenty-seven of *Raglan*'s crew had been killed out of a complement of 220 and *M28* had lost eight out of sixty-six. A court martial absolved the ship's companies of any blame but did criticise Admiral Hayes-Sadler for dividing his forces and leaving the monitors so exposed. In fact the action of the two German ships, brave as it was, resulted in more damage to their cause than to the British. *Goeben* and *Breslau* were far more valuable to the Germans than the two monitors – designed to be expendable – were to the British. The Central Powers had lost their only serious naval assets (apart from U-boats) in the eastern Mediterranean, and the British were able to re-deploy old battleships and cruisers, no longer needed for *Goeben* watch, elsewhere.

Compared with the eastern Aegean, other stations for monitors in the Mediterranean theatre were uneventful. The two 12 inch monitors and some of the small ships were employed in the Adriatic (see map 5). Here Italy was locked in a struggle with Austria for control of territory bordering the Gulf of Trieste. The monitors were requested by the Italians to engage the Austrian forces near to Trieste itself. This was dangerously close to the Austrian fleet head-quarters at Pola. The Italians themselves were building some heavily gunned barges, but they were so slow and un-seaworthy as to be almost useless. *Picton* and *Peterborough* arrived in Venice in March 1917, *Picton* having the unique honour for a British naval vessel of an armoured train escort up the Italian coast. In May 1918 they supported the Italians in the 10th Battle of the Isonzo, bombarding Austrian railway communications and an airfield at Prosecco. Their firing was impressively effective and they escaped with minimal damage, except for one bomb which wounded the commanding admiral, Mark Kerr. One Austrian aircraft was badly damaged in the air and later shot down.

In August the 11th Battle of the Isonzo gave them another chance to show their mettle. They attacked entrenched posi-tions, ammunition dumps and communications, supporting an assault by Italian ground troops. They had their own spotting aircraft which was guarded by fighters. The bombardment was successful in doing extensive damage but Italian infantry could make only limited progress against well dug in opposition. Two of the Italian armed barges joined the foray, but with little effect.

In October the Austrians responded with the great Caporetto offensive. The monitors were called upon to evacuate Grado of personnel and guns, and they did this successfully in spite of worsening weather which forced the Italian barges ashore. The Italians held the Austrian advance on the River Piave, just east of Venice. The Austrians renewed their attack in November and the monitors were sent up the San Felice Channel, right on the front line. Their mission was to destroy pontoon bridges across the Piave. These were difficult targets as the bridges were small and the spotter aircraft were continually harassed by enemy fighters. At ranges on 19,000 to 15,000 yards, hits were obtained however. Eventually the Austrian offensive ran out of steam and the monitors returned south to refit. Their next and final assignation was to Albania to support Allied forces ranged against the Bulgarians and Austrians. Again an effective enfilading fire was brought down and the Italian commander on the spot commended their shooting.

The monitors had played a useful role in the campaign, especially in view of the chronic shortage of heavy artillery suffered by the Italians. Luckily for them the Austrian fleet had not intervened in their actions, and Austrian aircraft had been unable to do much damage. As we shall see, their sister 12 inch monitors were to experience much more testing conditions in their campaign on the Belgian coast.

Chapter 5

With the Dover Patrol

The Dover Patrol was one of the most active naval commands throughout the whole course of the war, and became, from 1916 onward, the main area for monitor activity. There were three commanding admirals during the war, Horace Hood, under whom *Severn, Mersey* and *Humber* had done such splendid work in 1914. Hood was then moved to command a battle cruiser squadron and replaced by Sir Reginald Bacon who commanded between 1915 and the end of 1917. Bacon was an exceptionally able officer, highly technically competent and always keen to try something new. Unfortunately he was also extremely stubborn, secretive and wilful to the point of insubordination. This led to his dismissal in December 1917 and replacement by Sir Roger Keyes. Keyes, who we have already encountered in the Dardanelles, was an almost hyper-active fire eater, a fine seaman and charismatic leader. Each of these leaders contributed something unique to the operations of the patrol, and each faced fearsome challenges in trying to rise to the multifarious demands placed upon him.

The Dover Strait itself is one of the most used waterways in the world, and remained so throughout the war. Control of it was vital to the whole war effort. Any Allied or neutral shipping approaching northern Europe or the east coast of Britain was compelled to pass through it during the war in order to be directed to a safe passage through the minefields in the North Sea and to be examined for contraband cargo which might otherwise find its way to Germany. Neutral ships were forced to anchor in the Downs, between Deal and the Goodwin Sands, to be inspected by men of the Inspection Service who came under the command of Dover. The Dover Patrol also had the job of overseeing the constant stream of war traffic across the channel, supplying men and munitions to the armies in France. Protecting this traffic from enemy U-boats and destroyers was a vital task, and any failure could have been fatal to the Allied cause. It entailed protecting the ports of Calais, Dunkirk, Dover, Folkestone and Boulogne from surface and underwater attack and from mines. This required constant aggressive patrolling of the Strait. Equally vital was to intercept enemy submarines trying to get down Channel to attack ships in the western approaches. This was important from the start of the war, but became absolutely critical from mid 1916 onward, when unrestricted submarine warfare came within an ace of forcing Britain out of the war. Allied to this duty was the laying and maintenance of mine-fields and nets in various parts of the Channel and off the Belgian coast, and sweeping enemy mines laid by surface vessels and submarines. The French and Belgian armies holding the left of the Allied line were in constant fear of a German landing from the sea behind their lines. This could easily cut them off and lead to a serious defeat. One heavy gunned ship had to be constantly employed to guard against the possibility of a small fleet of barges stealing along the coast, laden with German troops. All these defensive duties would have been enough for any man to handle, but they were only a part of the job of the admiral commanding Dover. As we shall see in some detail there were schemes for aggressive action in support of the armies on land, covering the seaward flank of any advance, breaking up enemy attacks, and landing our own troops behind the front line. Naval guns sometimes had to be dismounted, landed, transported inland and used to support hard pressed French and Belgian forces. The ports of Ostend, Zeebrugge and the inland port of Bruges became important bases for German surface craft and U-boats and could not be left alone, they had to be constantly harassed by gunfire, submarines and mines. At the same time the patrol was tasked to tie down as much enemy artillery and personnel as possible by bombarding the coastline, targeting coastal towns, communications and troop concentrations. Finally, in case all this was not enough to worry about, the patrol had to allocate ships to try to shoot down Zeppelins approaching up the Thames Estuary. In all these tasks the monitors played an important part.

The waters covered by the patrol are narrow and in some places extremely dangerous. Near the western entrance there are shallow banks, dangerous to large ships, and the Goodwin Sands, east of Dover, dry out at low water. The Belgian coast is featureless from seaward but is protected by a maze of sandbanks with only a few feet of water over them, making the coast very dangerous to approach except through a few deep channels and rendering safe navigation very difficult. The deep channels were of course subject to enemy mining and were pre-registered targets for long range coastal guns. Navigation marks, vital to peace time navigation, were liable to be removed or misleadingly re-moored. Tides run notoriously strongly in the Dover Strait, making 3-4 knots at springs. Off the Belgian coast they have the nasty habit of running across the channels between the shallows, doing their best to drive ships onto the banks. Tides of this strength make life extremely difficult for a clumsy monitor capable of only 5 knots. In westerly or south westerly winds, blowing up the channel from the Atlantic, the seas become extremely rough, breaking heavily in the shallow water, especially when the wind is against the tide. A winter northerly sends an icy blast down the North Sea which can easily drive an underpowered or disabled ship ashore on the Belgian coast. The area is also subject to frequent fogs and haze, adding to the difficulty of navigation.

When studying of the fortunes and misfortunes of the monitors, these sea conditions have to be constantly kept in mind. It is impossible not to admire the seamanship, courage and dogged fortitude of their crews.

From early 1915 until the end of the war, bombardment by big gun ships was virtually the only aggressive activity which the Royal Navy could undertake in home waters. The Grand Fleet at Scapa was in a posture of deterrence only, the German High Seas Fleet would in no circumstances risk a head on battle in the North Sea so there was little for the fleet to do but maintain its superiority. The only exception to this was the brief period of the Battle of Jutland which brought about no change in the relative strengths of the two battle fleets. The Harwich Force of light cruisers and destroyers made an effective sortie into the Heligoland Bight in 1914, but changes in German practices and extended minefields made another such action impossible. Naval strategy became almost entirely focused on defensive measures designed to intercept any attempt by the German fleet to put to sea, enforcing the distant blockade on Germany, anti-submarine warfare, minesweeping and deterring enemy layers and minesweepers. The Germans were able to be more aggressive, not only in sinking ships with U-boats and mines but also in carrying out ineffective but annoying raids with their cruisers on the east coast of England. The only place at which the navy could strike back was the Belgian coast. Even this was not easy. Belgium was an ally with an army fighting alongside British and French troops on the western front. Although only a very small part of the country remained unoccupied by the enemy, a large part of the Belgian Army was intact and also the Belgian royal family had close ties with Britain. Whatever the navy did, it had to be done with minimal Belgian civilian casualties. Any bombardment had to be pin point accurate and concentrated on German forces on or near the coast. This was at first especially challenging as the navy had not acquired much experience in shore bombardment before 1914 and had to learn the techniques involved "on the job".

The requirement to avoid hitting innocent civilians at first precluded the use of an alternative weapon for shore bombardment to the monitors, the bombing aircraft. The Royal Naval Air Service was in the forefront of aircraft development, vigorously encouraged by Churchill. Bases for RNAS aircraft under command of the Dover Patrol were established at Dover and Dunkirk, with numerous disbursed airfields nearby. The machines available in 1914 however carried only 20lb bombs which were pathetically ineffective, and aiming was so inaccurate that they could not possibly be used anywhere near where Belgian civilians might be. As the war progressed great strides were made in bombing techniques and machines. Short seaplanes were the first effective naval bombers to be used for coastal bombardment, these could carry bomb loads of up to 520lb and were fitted with a relatively efficient bomb sight. Shorts and Caudron seaplanes were used to bombard the harbours at Ostend and Zeebrugge, Zeppelin sheds, and the large gun emplacements on the coast. They were succeeded by land based Handley Page heavy bombers. For their day these were excellent machines, large, sturdy and reliable, with a normal load of twelve 112lb bombs. They became available to the Dover Patrol in mid 1917 and from that time onward played a significant part in the Belgian coast campaign, but were never anything like as effective against protected targets as was naval gunfire.

Nelson is supposed to have said that "Only a fool attacks land fortifications from the sea," – although the truth is that he effectively did exactly that himself several times. This was of course just what the monitors were required to do throughout the course of the war. Their task was about as difficult as it is possible to imagine. Apart from the problems of weather and sea conditions mentioned above, the Belgian coast is low lying and protected by sand dunes which make it difficult to see anything inland or to fix one's position at sea. As soon as the Germans occupied it, they set about building a series of formidable heavily armoured gun emplacements which were steadily increased in range and effectiveness as the war progressed. By 1918 the following batteries were in operation, their location is shown on the map 1, all of them were extremely well protected behind concrete and earthworks:

1 Bremen 4 x 4 inch
2 Lekkerbek n/a
3 Hamberg 6 x 4 inch
4 Kaiser 4 x 12 inch
5 Fresa 3 x 6 inch

6 Augusta 4 x 8 inch
7 Goeben 3 x 6 inch
8 The Mole 4 x 4 inch
9 The Mole 2 x 6 inch
10 Wurtemburg 4 x 4 inch
11 Grossen 4 x 11 inch Howitzers
12 Bellisch 4 x 5 inch
13 Donerklok 4 x 11 inch
14 Kaiserin 4 x 6 inch
15 Hafen 4 x 4 inch
16 Hertnan 4 x 8 inch
17 De Kaan 4 x 11 inch
18 Deutschland 4 x 15 inch
19 Turkijen 4 x 11 inch
20 Irene 3 x 6 inch
21 Hindenburg 4 x 11 inch
22 Frederich 4 x 4 inch
23 Eylau 4 x 4 inch
24 Palace 2 x 6 inch
25 Tirpitz 4 x 11 inch
26 Cecilie 4 x 6 inch
27 Oldenburg 4 x 6 inch
28 Baesler 4 x 6 inch
29 Antwerpen 5 x 4 inch
30 Achen 4 x 6 inch
31 No name 1 x 6 inch
32 Lengenboom 1 x 15 inch
33 – 36 No name 8 x 6 inch + 2 x 8 inch howitzers.

Never has a coast line been so heavily defended.

Obviously the combined fire power of these heavy guns far outweighed that of any combination of warships which might approach them. Also land based guns are always more effective than ship mounted guns. With rigid mountings in a known position they can be pre-registered on various points at sea, and they can be arranged to elevate much higher than is normal for naval guns, so optimising range. Hidden behind concrete and earthworks they are almost impossible to put out of action and their ammunition can be buried deep underground, away from any danger. By contrast a single heavy gun hit anywhere on a ship, especially a fairly lightly armoured ship like a monitor, can easily put it out of action. Ships are of course normally a moving target, although this was often not the case with monitors, movement makes ships more difficult to hit, but at the same time makes it harder for them to take accurate aim. Any swell will make the ship roll, which is a major additional complication. Unlike coastal guns, bombarding ships are always vulnerable to attack from destroyers, torpedo boats or aircraft which may damage them or force them to give up the bombardment entirely. Altogether the odds are weighted against them, confirming the good sense in Nelson's dictum.

As it was almost never possible to see the target which monitors were engaging on the Belgian coast, because of smoke or the coastal sand dunes, it was normally necessary to have some form of spotter communicating with the ship. In the bombardments carried out by the ex-Brazilian monitors in 1914 this could be done by artillery officers on the ground, but as soon as the front stabilised, this became more difficult. For a time it was possible to observe gunfire from tall buildings on shore behind the friendly lines, but these were never very well placed to take cross bearings, and anyway most of the tall buildings were knocked down by artillery quite early on. It was plain that other methods had to be devised. The most amazing of these was Admiral Bacon's tripods. These were movable steel structures built of railway rails bolted together as necessary. The main legs sat on the sea bottom forming a triangle with 23 foot sides. The working platform was a steel U-channel on which were perched two observing officers, two signalmen and their kit, which included accurate bearing compasses, signal flags and oxy-acetylene lamps. The total height was 44 feet, of which about 35 was normally under water when the towers were in use. The total area of the platform was 6 foot 9 inches by 5 foot 4 inches, so it must have been a crowded situation in which to work, as well as a hair raising one. Two platforms were used at a time, being transported on colliers with powerful winches which could get them into position quickly. They would be carried up quite close to the enemy coast during the hours of darkness, ready for action at first light. As they were quite small they would be unlikely to be spotted by the enemy. On the tripods the observers could see both the target and the fall of shot. Men on each tripod would take a bearing on the fall of shot and signal corrections to the monitor, several miles away out to sea. When the shoot was over, the colliers, covered by destroyers and a smoke screen, would steam in and collect the tripods and their doubtless much relieved crews. Much time was spent developing this technique but it was never very successful because the towers were not high enough to give a really good view, and the whole procedure was obviously fraught with risk.

Another method of spotting involved kite balloons. A kite balloon was a hydrogen filled balloon large enough to lift one or two people with field glasses, telephone equipment and maps. The observers in the balloon would identify targets then spot for the guns below. These were much used by land based artillery and were tried on ships, but there were many difficulties. A ship large enough to carry a balloon inflated had to be found and then the inflated balloon would be launched and towed into position by a trawler. Strong winds or hazy conditions would obviously make it useless, and invariably it would be a tempting target for enemy aircraft. Altogether balloons took too long to get into position and were too unreliable for use at sea, they were consequently rarely used on ships undertaking coastal bombardment. The enemy coastal batteries however used them extensively to spot targets at sea. They would be tethered quite close to the gun position and protected by high angle anti-aircraft guns and machine guns. Sometimes fighter aircraft would also be detailed to protect them. Royal Naval Air Service fighters devised all sorts of methods for bringing them down. As incendiary bullets for the Lewis guns normally carried on "scouts" (as fighters were often called at the time) were seldom available, one method for knocking out balloons involved using Le Prieur rockets which were explosive light artillery weapons. They were fired electrically. Two of them would be attached to the inter wing struts of a small aircraft which would try to get directly above the balloon, at an altitude above the effective range of the defensive guns. The aircraft would then dive vertically down on it letting loose the rockets 3-400 feet from the target. At any longer range than this the rockets would veer off course and miss the balloon. This tactic made the attacking aircraft difficult for anti-aircraft fire to hit but was extremely demanding on the nerves of the pilot. In the dive the plane would reach 200 mph or more, a fearful speed for the time, and pulling out of the dive was very liable to wrench the wings off the machine. On one occasion a pioneer of this method, Flight Sub Lieutenant

Mackenzie, actually left the release of his rocket so late that he was under the balloon when it exploded and he came within an ace of hitting the falling cable as the balloon plunged to earth from just above him. Once their spotting balloon was shot down the coastal guns would normally have to stop firing.

Much more promising than balloons was the use of aircraft. Quite early in the war the navy set about to develop a camera suitable for finding targets and assessing damage done by bombardments, this was not easy given the poor performance of aircraft of the time, and all sorts of gimcrack ideas were put forward. Eventually Admiral Bacon himself sent an officer to London to trawl round all the optical shops he could find and buy the biggest and best lens he could get, paying for it with the admiral's own money. He re-appeared with two 8 inch lenses costing some £120, a huge sum in those days, and a camera was built round them in naval workshops. It was mounted on a double gimbal arrangement so that it constantly faced downwards whatever the altitude of the aircraft. This proved to be a great step forward enabling proper pictures of coastal defences to be taken. It was first used in July 1916 to record damage done to the powerful *Tirpitz* battery during an attack by monitors. Eventually a 20-inch lens was found and with further modifications to the camera excellent results were obtained. Even more difficult was to get a radio system to work properly in a spotting aircraft and communicate reliably with ships. As early as 1912 the Admiralty had experimented with simple radio sets in seaplanes and by 1914 HMS *Vernon,* the Royal Navy's signals and research centre, had developed a 660 watt radio transmitter for aircraft. This worked on the synchronous spark system and had a range of up to 30 miles. We have already

seen how effectively these could be used to direct the guns of
Mersey and *Severn* onto a small invisible target. Initially the
sets could only send signals, not receive them, making the
system extremely difficult to use. By 1916 transmitter/receiver
sets were available but it was far from easy to listen to and
operate a wireless set in the open cockpit of a primitive aeroplane. All the signalling was of course in Morse code and the
observing aeroplane was likely to be being thrown about by
air currents and at the same time had to keep out of the way
of enemy fighters and hope not to be hit by ground fire, so
the signaller's job was not an enviable one. However the
RNAS did eventually work out a viable method for using a
single machine to spot for several ships. Ships would fire so
as to leave 20 second intervals between each shot, and would
buzz an identity code to the aeroplane at the moment of firing.
The observer would know the approximate flight time of the
shell and would watch for it to burst. He would have studied
aerial photographs of the target area and know exactly what
the gun was aiming at – perhaps a lock gate, a railway junction, or an enemy battery. He would buzz the ship as soon as
he saw the burst then give details of where it had landed in
relation to the aiming point, say three o'clock, 100 yards. The
gun would then correct its aim and try again. This may sound
relatively simple, but it took a lot of practice and extremely
steady nerves (and a strong stomach) to do it correctly. The
flight time of a shell would often be 30 seconds or more (a shell
typically travelled at 2,500 feet/second – about 1,700 mph – at
20,000 yards range the flight time would be about 24 seconds),
so the observer would be reporting the fall of one shell while
the next was in the air. Observation aircraft were almost
always protected by fighters which often resulted in fierce air
battles over the Belgian coast.

However good the observation might be, it was most important to get shots on target as soon as possible, not only to reduce ammunition wastage but also because the enemy would quickly make life as difficult as possible for the observer by using smoke, jamming radio signals, or attacking the observers in their aeroplane. Also the shorter the bombardment the less time the enemy would have to bring down effective fire on the monitor offshore.

It is easy in the days of satellite positioning systems, to forget the difficulties of accurate navigation which beset warships in the early part of the twentieth century. In order to aim at a target on shore which it cannot see, a ship must know exactly where it is itself and the precise location of the target. The coastal waters of Belgium had last been surveyed in the 1840s and there had been many changes since then, and in any case a slow moving ship like a monitor, subject to tidal streams, had great difficulty in knowing exactly where it was. The technique eventually developed was for a trawler to lay a large buoy in the selected spot then a destroyer would drop two depth charges close to it. Sound detecting systems in England could get accurate cross bearings on the buoy to establish its exact position and the monitor would anchor close to it, thus knowing exactly where it was. There was a downside to this arrangement in that the Germans also had sophisticated listening equipment and could use this to work out where the ship would be for the next bombardment so as to register their guns on that precise spot. This in turn was foxed by the practice of dropping pairs of depth charges frequently even if no attack was going to take place, thus confusing the enemy gun crews. Accurate fixing of the position of targets on shore was another problem, as maps of the shore could not easily be reconciled with charts and in any case gun emplacements sometimes moved and often sprung up in new locations. Accurate maps compatible with ship's charts had to be made and constantly revised based on aerial photography. Having fixed the ship's position and that of the target, the monitors had to find a fixed reference point for the gun sight to aim at. The gun sights themselves were in the turrets of the small monitors, but the larger ships all had director towers from which the guns were aimed, the chief gunnery officer in the tower established the angle and range settings which were then transmitted to the turrets where the gun crews would use them to lay their weapons. A reference point was needed on which the sights would be trained and the guns would be pointed on a bearing referred to that point. As there were almost no visible features on the Belgian shore, a small monitor usually sailed with each large monitor and anchored a distance away (normally 4-6 miles depending on visibility) to act as the reference point. It could also make itself useful by chasing away any enemy destroyers with its heavy armament. If the large monitor was to fire while under way a constant bearing had to be taken on the reference point and for this purpose a device called Gyro Director Training Gear was eventually developed and fitted to all the large monitors. Occasionally the army would ask the monitors to fire at night on an area where enemy troops were known to be resting. For this a special technique was developed and used until the Gyro Director Training Gear was fitted in 1918 (see figure 9). An imaginary line was marked on the sea, say 15,000 yards from the target area, each end of the line is marked by a ship showing a bright light. A third lighted ship would be anchored opposite the target and 15,000 yards to seaward of the line. The monitor would steam slowly along the line with her sights trained on the third lighted ship, but with the controls of the director reversed so that instead of firing at the third ship it would be firing directly away from it, that is to say exactly at the target. Obviously this arrangement left a good deal of scope for error, and at night it was impossible to spot the fall of shot, but as the target would be troops camped over a large area in the open country, accuracy was not so critical.

Even when the position of the ship and the target were known, getting the correct gun elevation for range setting was a further challenge. There were of course the normal variable features of the guns themselves, especially when they were worn, and of the ammunition. Wind, humidity and a host of other factors also had to be taken into account. To allow for the different characteristics of each individual gun and its state of wear, range tables were made up for each barrel giving the angle of elevation to be used for each selected range. These were made up during practice shoots. However guns were not gyro stabilised and so if the ship was rolling, getting the range right was very difficult. Initially this was done simply by eye, but eventually an automatic gyro system was developed which actually triggered the gun at the precise moment when the ship was on an even keel. To reduce rolling as much as possible, supporting ships such as destroyers were ordered not to dash around anywhere near the monitors in action except in emergencies, as their wash could cause ships to roll in calm weather.

Bacon, who took over the Dover Patrol in April 1915, was something of an artillery expert, having been Managing Director of the Coventry Ordinance Works during a break from his naval service. He had also commanded heavy howitzers and shore based naval guns in France in the early stages of the war. He was naturally keen to start a programme of coastal bombardment as soon as possible. At first the only heavy gun ship available to him was the old battleship *Revenge* which had 12 inch guns with a range of 16,000 yards. She was fitted with anti-torpedo bulges. *Revenge* was quite unsuitable for coastal work as she drew 26 feet of water. The very short range of her guns could be increased by flooding one of the bulges so as to heel her over, but in this condition the upper side of the hull of course had no torpedo protection. Her main role was to help in developing bombardment techniques. In particular she did valuable work developing techniques for working with spotting aircraft. Deprived of the 14 inch monitors and of the first two 12 inch ships, all of which, as we have seen, went off to the Dardanelles, Bacon had to wait until August 1915 before he had a force of three 12 inch ships available (*Lord Clive, Sir John Moore* and *Prince Rupert*). He immediately sent them off to a training ground in the Thames Estuary where some of the features of the Belgian coast had been reproduced. The results at first were a grave disappointment. Apart from the ship's slow speed and poor handling their "second hand" guns and turrets were very unreliable, continually bursting the ancient copper hydraulic pipes which powered the gun turrets and suffering from numerous mechanical problems. After several weeks they were patched up so that the ships were ready to work in conjunction with the newly constructed tripods. Bacon was very much concerned with the vulnerability of these large, slow, ships, close to the harbours of Ostend and Zeebrugge which were infested with powerful enemy destroyers and submarines, so quite an armada was prepared to protect them. There were drifters, no less than sixty of them, to lay anti-torpedo nets round the big ships, trawlers hunting enemy mines, ten destroyers, colliers to carry the tripods, a seaplane carrier, an armed yacht and tugs in case of emergencies. The shallow water to the shoreward side of the bombarding ships made an attack from that direction unlikely, but Bacon was an ex commander of the Royal Navy's submarine force and knew how dangerous it would be if the U-boats worked round to the seaward side of the monitors. The drifters therefore had to lay a "zareba", or barrier, of mined nets to protect the firing zone. This consisted of 16 miles of net arranged in a complicated triangular pattern. The laying of this was carried out by civilian fishermen, working in the dark, under naval orders. The fishermen showed astonishing skill and fortitude.

The weather and tidal conditions had to be just right to give this sort of operation a reasonable chance of success. The sea had to be reasonably smooth, visibility good, and the tide had to be suitable to allow the tripods to be used without getting swamped or left projecting too high above the surface. After a false start on 21 August, cancelled as the sea was too rough for the colliers, this extraordinary force, rudely christened "Fred Kano's Navy", consisting of about 100 ships, set sail on 22 August and rendezvoused at the Galloper Light near the mouth of the Thames. It then set off at about 6 knots across the North Sea. The first waypoint was the West Hinder light, which was reached without incident, from there the force split in two, the collier selected to position the eastern tripod, accompanied by two destroyers forged on towards Knoke, while the rest of the force turned south westward towards their station directly opposite Zeebrugge. A torpedo boat had been sent on ahead of the main party to lay lighted buoys marking the ends of a shoal (they couldn't be found as the sandbanks had shifted) and to establish reference points for the bombarding ships.

Although no one knew much about the defensive batteries, on this occasion the monitors were to fire whilst at anchor, risking being hit by the coastal guns. Fire was to be opened at dawn. The target was the lock gates at Zeebrugge, and industrial works near the harbour. The bombardment was disappointingly ineffective. Sir *John Moore,* (on which Bacon himself was embarked) suffered a rupture of some pipework after nine rounds and had to cease fire, on *Prince Rupert* a failed electrical circuit broke the link between the director tower and the gun turret so orders had to be transmitted by voice reducing the rate of fire and causing confusion. She consequently only got off nineteen rounds. *Lord Clive* performed better and kept up her bombardment for one and three quarter hours firing thirty-one rounds at the lock and eleven at the works. Range was about 18,000 yards, just outside the effective range of the coastal guns at that time (16,000 yards). As the tide began to flood, threatening to submerge the tripods, the operation ceased, the nets were picked up, and the ramshackle armada plodded off home. The enemy had attempted to shell the tripod laying ships but missed them. Their shells also landed well short of the bombarding monitors. It was difficult at the time to know how much damage was done to the locks or the factories. Photo reconnaissance suggested several ships, including two U-boats, and some harbour installations at Zeebrugge, damaged, but post war research did not confirm many of these claims. There were certainly several near misses of the lock gates, and two barges were sunk. Had the lock gates been disabled the enemy would have been severely disadvantaged, because Bruges was being established as a major U-boat base, the boats gaining access to the sea via the Bruges-Zeebrugge Canal and its locks. In truth it was very optimistic to expect to hit such a tiny target as a lock gate at such a long range. Minor damage was caused to the industrial works close to the harbour. Bacon claimed to be rather disappointed that neither U-boats nor destroyers attempted to attack his force, as he had hoped to bag a few of each. In spite of the rather unsatisfactory result, the astonishing aspect of this operation will be readily understood by anyone who has had to arrange any sort of maritime operation in the dark. It must have taken brilliant staff work to get all these ships and their attendant tripods, nets and mines in the correct position exactly on time and the scope for disastrous mistakes is easy to imagine. Bacon's powers of organisation and the seamanship of his subordinates is astonishing, particularly in the light of the fact that the operation had had to be postponed for twenty-four hours on account of the weather.

From this first raid the Germans learnt that they must install much more effective coastal artillery and strengthen their power to retaliate. The Royal Navy learnt lessons too:

- The monitors needed a lot more working up;
- Shore bombardment was perfectly possible;
- The enemy seemed reluctant to attack the bombarding force by sea.

The next attack was planned for 5 September. Once again the weather intervened so the convoy left on 6th, this time passing close to Dunkirk, in case the enemy should be expecting an attack by the northern route used in August. The target selected was the dockyards at Ostend which were being used by enemy destroyers to harass ships in the southern North Sea. A diversionary raid was to be made on

Westende, a few miles down the coast by the old battleship *Redoubtable* together with the gunboats *Excellent* and *Bustard*. The observation tripods were to be used again and the mined nets would be laid to protect the attackers. Bacon was aware that at least two 11 inch guns were installed at Ostend and was certain that these would prove to be a formidable danger. He therefore decreed that the bombardment would take place with the monitors under way. In the event it was just as well that he did. *Moore* was at Chatham having her faulty turrets seen to, but *Crauford* had arrived from the builders so she, *Clive*, *Rupert* and *M25* (9.2 inch small monitor) made up the bombarding force. Bacon flew his flag in *Clive*.

At first light on 7th the eighty-seven ships, which this time comprised the armada, and the tripods, were positioned in perfectly clear weather. Just before fire could be opened however a mist came down and completely obscured the target. After waiting for half an hour the main force withdrew to watch the diversionary bombardment by *Redoubtable*, the weather over Westende being quite clear. On the way they were attacked by aircraft which managed to hit and damage *Attentive*, a light cruiser acting as a destroyer leader. Two men were killed and six others injured. This was one of the very few occasions when a bomb made a hit on a moving ship. Early in the afternoon the fog lifted, so the monitors and their attendants returned to their firing position about 18,000 yards off shore. Immediately they saw an enemy kite balloon go up from behind the batteries on shore, indicating the possibility of effective counter fire. This indeed proved to be the case. Almost immediately a heavy shell crashed into the water close to *Crauford* making it apparent that not only had the enemy quickly found the range, but that their battery was even more formidable than expected. It was indeed. These were the first shots from the four 11 inch guns of the *Tirpitz* battery which was to be the bane of the monitors for the rest of the war. It was firing regularly every two minutes, and getting uncomfortably close. Bacon signalled a withdrawal to 19,500 yards. He found that as he opened the range the battery ceased to fire salvoes, but methodically followed the ships with one gun only so as to establish the exact range, economising on ammunition. It seemed that the gunners had also guessed that the leading monitor, *Clive,* must be the flagship and concentrated their fire on her. At 19,500 yards the monitors fell into line and opened fire, all the time being strafed by *Tirpitz* now firing full four gun salvoes. The tripods were by this time almost under water, due to the rising tide, and not useable for spotting, but instead two Short seaplanes belonging to the carrier *Riviera* were able to spot effectively, while at the same time some observation posts behind the Allied lines on shore provided useful information. *Clive* was hit four times, one shell struck her bulge, doing little damage, another hit a 3 pounder gun on deck. The gun was sent skimming across the deck, and several men were hurt, but luckily the 11 inch shell did not explode and simply shattered. Another shot carried away the flag halyards which fell on deck entangling Bacon's chief of staff, Captain Browning, in coils of light line. A block from the top of the halyard struck another officer on the head causing a serious injury. The fourth struck her bows doing no serious damage. The trajectory of the shells indicated that the guns were elevated to a high angle which brought the danger of one plunging through the lightly armoured deck into the bowels of the ship. It was clear to Bacon that his ships were in severe danger, so he signalled a further withdrawal.

The enemy guns followed him up to a range of 22,000 yards, making the retreat distinctly uncomfortable. The monitors could not fire back as their turrets would only train forwards. Suddenly at 22,000 yards the enemy fire ceased. The reason, it was later discovered, was not because the guns could reach no further but because a premature detonation caused a shell fired by the battery to fall short, landing very close to the gun emplacement itself and doing damage, which forced the battery to use reduced charges, enabling the monitors to make good their escape.

There were some dramas related to the tripods. One used at Westende was seen and badly shot up by the enemy and had to be evacuated under fire. The others were rapidly becoming submerged and had to be left behind. This was a consequence of the whole operation having been delayed by the morning fog. Unfortunately it enabled the enemy to lift the tripods and understand their function, so they could not be used in future as they would be a prime target for the smaller coastal guns. In place of the evacuated tripod, a kite balloon towed by a trawler was used to spot the fall of shot for the ships firing at Westende.

The results of this second day of action were mixed. The British had suffered a handful of casualties and there was some minor damage. *Crauford* and *Clive* had been hit, but not seriously damaged and off Westende *Redoubtable* had suffered two 6 inch gun hits, again not suffering serious damage. In return there had been some damage done to the dockyard. On 18 September there was another attack on Westende, without any significant result. It was now clear to Bacon that the 12 inch monitors by themselves did not have the range to handle the shore batteries. To make an effective attack he would require bigger guns. He did not have long to wait. On 3 September, *Marshal Ney*, the first (and worst) of the horribly unsatisfactory 15 inch monitors, limped into Shoeburyness to calibrate her guns. She had travelled down from the Tyne with great difficulty, struggling all the way with her unreliable MAN diesel engines. If the Germans on the Belgian coast had a sense of humour, and if they knew anything about the tribulations of poor *Marshall Ney*, they would have had a good laugh for the next few weeks.

In late September, General, Sir John French, in command of the British Army in France, asked Bacon to put on a show of force on the coast to draw forces away from a planned assault he hoped to make further south. Bacon responded by devising a tactic which he thought would bluff the enemy and lead him to expect a coastal landing behind their lines. To do this he would bombard not the lock gates and harbours but the coastal batteries themselves, giving the impression that he was preparing the way for an amphibious assault. He split his forces into two squadrons. One consisting of the 12 inch monitors *Prince Eugene* and *General Crauford* with five destroyers, two paddle minesweepers, the armed yacht *Sandra* and attendant drifters, would attack gun emplacements near Zeebrugge; the other with *Ney, Wolfe, Clive* and *Moore* would try to tackle the formidable batteries at Ostend. For this action much faith was being placed on the untried 15 inch guns of *Ney* which should be able to out range the coastal artillery.

The ships set off from Dunkirk on 19 September. The Zeebrugge squadron experienced heavy counter fire, during which the yacht *Sandra* was sunk. With her went a remarkable officer, Lieutenant Commander Tipping. He was well over 70 years old, long retired from the navy, but he had insisted on returning to active service and started

1 HMS *Humber*

This picture shows *Humber* in her original configuration. Later she had a second turret with a single 6 inch gun mounted on the after deck, and the 4.5 inch howitzers were moved onto the upper deck. It is easy to see that her designers intended her for riverine use only. Any sort of sea would swamp the lower decks, and her lack of draft would cause her to skid sideways in a crosswind. However her low profile made her a difficult target and she and her sisters all survived the war with no serious damage.

2 HMS *Gorgon*

Built as a coastal defence vessel for Norway, *Gorgon* was a well designed and seaworthy ship and could achieve excellent long range shooting with her two single 9.2 inch turrets. She was able to elevate her main armament forty degrees giving a range of 39,000 yards. Unlike other monitors she could engage targets at long range with her after gun when she was opening the range. Unfortunately she did not come into service until 1918, due to many modifications to the original Norwegian design required by the Admiralty. Had she been in service earlier she might have been a very important asset to the Dover Patrol's forces engaging coastal guns in occupied Belgium.

3 HMS *Abercrombie* (1914)

This picture shows the stark, uncluttered layout of the 14 inch monitors. Note the side bulges and the high gunnery control tower at the top of the tripod mast. Her 14 inch main armament was manufactured by Bethlehem Steel for battle cruisers to be delivered to Greece, which became redundant when war broke out. *Abercrombie* had quite an active war in the Mediterranean, covering the Gallipoli operations and various Allied operations in the Aegean. On one occasion she managed to fire her anti-aircraft gun into a store on petrol on deck, causing a severe fire. Luckily the damage was minor.

4 HMS *Lord Clive*

Clive was one of the 12 inch monitors, originally fitted with 12 inch guns removed from obsolete battleships, onto which a massive 18 inch turret was mounted in 1918. This monstrous weapon came too late to be much used, and one wonders how long the structure of the ship could stand the recoil of the great gun. The 18 inch turret only had fifteen degrees of traverse, so the whole ship had to be correctly aligned before the gun could be aimed. Its recoil would cause her to skid sideways, dragging her anchors or even breaking the chain. The presence of a powerful tug was essential. No other ships in the Royal Navy have ever been fitted with such huge guns. In their normal configuration the 12 inch monitors did not have the range to engage German shore batteries successfully but were useful for net defence work and general patrol operations in the Channel.

5 HMS *Soult*

The picture clearly shows the astonishing layout of the first generation of 15 inch monitors. The conning tower just forward of the great gun turret must have given the officer of the watch a very poor view of what was going on. The navigator was located in the lower "bird's nest" on the tripod mast. His compass faithfully followed the alignment of the guns when they traversed, making his job extremely difficult. *Soult* had two Vickers four stroke 750 horsepower diesels, which proved economical and reliable but were totally insufficient for a ship of her size and bulk. She could barely manage 6 knots. The windage of her upper-works and her underpowered engines made her extremely difficult to steer, causing many minor bumps when going into harbour and often resulting in the ship spinning round without warning when steaming in a strong wind. She was, however a very useful bombardment ship and did some excellent work on the Belgian coast. Her 15 inch turret was reliable and some of her firing was commendably accurate.

6 HMS *Erebus* in 1919

Probably the best known and the longest lived of the British monitors, *Erebus* is shown here at a buoy off Dover during the First World War. She retains some of the strange features of the first 15 inch monitors but has finer lines and 6,000 horsepower as opposed to *Soult's* 1,500. Note that the conning tower has given place to a bridge above the turret structure. As first built she was able to achieve 14 knots. During the course of the Second World War she was fitted with a complex array of radars and secondary armament and a mizzen mast. All this extra top hamper slowed her down and made her very unhandy and difficult to control. She was often something of a figure of fun in the 1940s on account of her age and low speed. In spite of her many problems and frequent breakdowns she was an extremely useful ship, proving her worth during the invasion of Sicily, in the Normandy landings and at Walcheren.

7 HMS *Roberts* (1941)

The second monitor to bear this name *Roberts* had a busy war in the Mediterranean and later off the Normandy beaches and at Walcheren. The design was very similar to that of the second generation of 15 inch monitors except that she was fitted with turbine engines giving 4,800 horsepower making her slightly slower than *Erebus* but much more economical, (2.2 tons of oil per hour at 12 knots, against 3.8). She also had a mizzen mast from the outset, anti-aircraft radar and an advanced fire control system. She was the last monitor to be scrapped, having been laid up in Portsmouth Harbour until 1965. Her finest hour was probably her D-Day bombardment of Sword Beach, where she effectively silenced a number of heavy enemy batteries until one of her gun barrels split.

8 Preparation for the Great Landing
One of Bacon's pontoons being attached to the bows of two 12 inch monitors, so as to be pushed against the sea wall near Ostend. The pontoons would be loaded with tanks, guns and troops, who would swarm ashore over the wall and meet up with British forces thrusting up from Ypres. Unfortunately the offensive on land made little progress and the landing was cancelled. The monitors found they could handle the 540 foot long pontoons quite well in calm weather. Their heavy guns were to fire over the heads of troops on the pontoons using reduced charge ammunition to reduce the effect of blast, even with these charges the effect of firing the guns would have been pretty horrific. Ahead of the pontoons shallow draft rafts would be deployed so that the troops could land almost dry shod, and special ramps were devised for the tanks which would lead the way over the wall.

9 In the White Sea
A small monitor crashes through the ice, forcing its way up river to support British troops fighting the Bolshevik forces in northern Russia. In spite of the excellent job done by these little ships the venture was a complete failure due to the disloyalty, poor leadership and bad organisation of White forces.

10 HMS *Terror* Subjected to a Bombing Raid

Terror completely wore out her guns whilst supporting the British advance in the desert in 1941. She was then relegated to anti-aircraft picket duties although she had no radar. She eventually succumbed to heavy raids by German dive bombers and had to be evacuated and sunk. During the campaign she had provided invaluable help to the advancing army by harassing enemy communications and making movement along the coastal roadways and through small towns extremely dangerous. She was able to suppress the Italian artillery allowing smaller gunboats and destroyers to operate close in shore. So successful was *Terror* in this role that the Royal Navy realised the potential of monitors to support amphibious operations in many subsequent amphibious landings. (From a painting by Lieutenant Commander R. Langmaid RN).

working with the Dover Patrol as soon as war broke out. Recognising his experience and enthusiasm, Bacon had given him command of *Sandra*. This squadron returned to Dunkirk each evening to replenish ammunition and kept up its bombardment intermittently until early October without further serious accident. It was attacked unsuccessfully by both aircraft and submarines, one torpedo from *U.17* being observed to pass cleanly under a monitor, proving once again the virtues of having a shallow draft. The squadron attacking Ostend had an exciting time. It was hoped that by approaching from close inshore the squadron could avoid the fire of the *Tirpitz* battery by being outside its arc of fire. This ruse did not work, but Bacon still hoped that *Ney's* 15 inch guns could out range the shore battery. She first opened fire at 15,000 yards but was forced to open the range after seven rounds, she then tried again from further in shore off La Panne, getting better results and actually causing the Aachen battery to be temporally abandoned, but at that moment of triumph her customary bad luck manifested itself. The shock of her main armament firing dislodged a pin securing her main anchor and as she was under way the chain ran out and secured itself firmly to the sea bottom stopping the ship with a jerk. The windlass failed to raise the anchor and the unfortunate ship found herself firmly secured to the bottom, under enemy fire. At the same time the starboard engine failed and the ship swung round and grounded on a sandbank. Just to make matters even worse the inadequate steering engine refused to move the rudder. There was only one thing to do. The chain was let go and abandoned together with the anchor. Bacon then ordered the ship to be towed away from the action by the destroyer *Viking* under cover of a smokescreen. It must have been the ultimate disgrace for a ship from which so much had been expected. The monitors were back at work again four days later, this time their target was Westende, *Ney* managed seventeen rounds before having to be towed away again with engine trouble. She was sent to Southampton for dry docking, leaving the 12 inch ships and the small monitors to continue the bombardment. No great damage was done to the enemy, but the Germans do seem to have been deceived into thinking that a landing was being planned, more troops were moved to the coast and the batteries were strength-ened. The coastal guns had managed to drive off the monitors, and enemy aircraft activity increased becoming a serious menace to the bombarding ships. The German airmen developed a technique of diving out of the setting sun so as to gain surprise, but their bomb aiming was not good and they did no major damage.

In spite of the success of the naval diversion tactic, the army's autumn offensive ground to a halt, as did offensive drives by both sides at this stage of the war. The combination of barbed wire, machine guns and counter fire from defending artillery, was too much for the attacking formations.

The monitor's attacks had been carried out with the bombarding ships under way and spotting was carried out by seaplane which now was able to communicate reasonably well with the monitors. Crews in the aircraft were actually able to see the great shells in flight towards their targets provided they themselves were flying low enough. Naturally they had to avoid getting too low or they might be in the path of a high trajectory shell. Several Royal Flying Corps aircraft seem to have been lost on the western front by flying too close to the path of heavy artillery shells. A 15 inch shell travelling at just over twice the speed of sound caused terrific shock waves which could destroy an aircraft, even if the projectile passed some distance away.

During October there were some further sporadic bombardments, some of which were effective in putting the coastal guns temporarily out of action, but fire had to be limited so as to conserve ammunition, and also because gun barrels had only a limited life and spares were extremely scarce. The monitor force had now been joined by the 15 inch *Soult*, and now consisted of six 12 inch ships and the two 15 inchers. Unlike *Ney*, *Soult* proved quite reliable, if terribly slow. By now a fairly regular routine had been established, with the ships working from the forward base at Dunkirk, one monitor being normally at sea outside the harbour to prevent any attempt by enemy destroyers or mine layers to interfere with cross channel traffic.

During December a number of important experiments were carried out by the monitor force. The first was to check how easy it would be to run monitors right up to the beach so as to carry out an amphibious landing. This involved steaming inshore, shortening the range and keeping up regular fire. The results indicated that this would be feasible, if risky. The second was to develop better methods of aerial spotting. To develop this, a bombardment of Westende was carried out with spotting both from on land, behind the Belgian lines, and from the air. A comparison between the two results showed that land based spotting was more accurate. It was obviously only possible to carry it out however when engaging targets a few miles from Allied lines. Improved techniques for aerial spotting were required and it was found that the best method was to get the observers extremely closely acquainted with the topography on land, using maps, photographs and practice flights, so they could judge the fall of shots more accurately. All these exercises had to be carried out at a series of different altitudes. Trials were also made using a prominent lighted aiming mark near La Panne which could reduce the need for using small monitors as aiming marks. Better procedures for adjusting aim following the instructions of aerial observers were also developed. Gunnery officers were instructed to make the full correction given by the observer if the shots were more than 300 yards of range or 50 yards of direction off target. If it was less that these distances off half the observer's, correction was to be applied. In practice this greatly improved results.

All this painstaking work was carried out in winter, under fire, close to strongly held enemy harbours and in conditions which might at any time call for all or part of the force to be withdrawn to face a threat to the cross channel traffic. It says a lot for Bacon's powers of leadership and organisation that it was successfully completed.

By January 1916 there was little the monitors could do on the Belgian coast until the promised new "properly designed" 15 inch ships appeared. *Soult*, the small monitors and the 12 inch monitors spent most of the winter and early spring on anti-Zeppelin duties in the Thames. This was really a propaganda exercise. The newspapers were outraged at the bombing of London and supposedly strategically important targets in Britain. In fact these raids were mere pinpricks, bomb aiming and navigation in airships was a pretty hit and miss affair, and in any case British intelligence had turned almost all of the agents who were supposed to be telling the enemy where strategic installations were. When a judge started to object to the way these traitors were being treated "Blinker" Hall, the chief of naval intelligence, threatened to give the Zeppelin command the co-ordinates of the judge's own house. The monitors in the Thames may have assuaged public opinion a little, and in reality that was all that they were intended to do. The technique used was simple. The small monitors tried to pick up the airships at long range with their searchlights and the great guns of the large monitors would then try to blast them with air bursting shrapnel. Not surprisingly this was totally ineffective.

Ney had been withdrawn to Portsmouth in disgrace then sent to Cowes, where White's shipyard, who had assembled her engines under licence from MAN, tried to put them right without any lasting success. She therefore had her 15 inch turret removed and 6 inch and 9.2 inch guns given to her instead. She was removed from normal duties and spent the rest of the war as guard ship at the important Downs anchorage. She did see some action even in this lowly role, once she was attacked by torpedo carrying seaplanes which fired at the large and barely mobile target and missed. On another occasion a strong patrol of powerful destroyers attempted to shell Ramsgate and attack shipping in the anchorage. *Ney*'s 6 inch guns were too much for them and they retired having done no serious damage. Nevertheless this was a sorry demotion for a ship in which the Admiralty had placed high hopes. It was of course entirely their lordship's own fault for forging ahead with untried technology resulting in an absurd piece of marine engineering, but with the mean and ungenerous spirit which typifies a government department when things go wrong, the Admiralty sought to blame the crew. This was manifestly unjust. Captain Hugh Tweedie, *Ney*'s captain, and his crew, made every possible effort to make their ship work, and Tweedie was famous throughout the Dover Patrol for his good humour in the face of adversities, but the Admiralty nevertheless punished the whole ship's company by discounting their time in *Ney* from their seniority in the navy.

Returning to the remainder of the monitor fleet, a brief attack was made around Westende in January 1916, using the newly developed techniques for spotting, this was in response from a request by the French to do whatever was possible to draw German forces away from the western front. It does not seem to have been particularly effective, as the monitors were not yet ready to challenge the enemy's heavy batteries. There were two duties however for which they were well suited. Mined anti-submarine nets were busily being laid in the southern North Sea to deter mine laying U-boats which were now the most serious threat to Allied shipping. No obstacle, however, is an obstacle for long unless it is covered by effective fire. That fire was provided by the 12 inch monitors and small monitors, which through the rest of the war patrolled the nets to prevent them from being destroyed or sunk by enemy destroyers and trawlers. It was dull, tough work, but there were sporadic bursts of activity which showed how effective a small ship with big guns could be against the most nimble destroyers.

Another mundane job was shipping large redundant naval guns to France for use as ultra-heavy artillery. Some old 12 inch guns and some 9.2 inch short range guns, removed from small monitors (where they were replaced by twin 6 inch turrets) were to be mounted in carefully concealed emplacements close to Dunkirk and arranged on inclined mountings to give them maximum range. Some of the largest components weighed over 100 tons and the largest cranes available would only lift 24 tons, so the weapons had to be transported on a shallow draft ship which could get right up to the quayside at high water, enabling the gigantic loads to be skidded onto special road trailers hauled by massive Daimler-Foster tractors. The only ship suitable for this was a 12 inch monitor, so *Crauford* found herself pressed into use as a ferry, carrying great gun barrels on her foredeck. The guns were supposed to be able to reach and harass the *Tirpitz* battery, in the event this was not achieved. The landing and mounting of the guns however was a great technical achievement for which Bacon himself must receive much of the credit.

1916 was of course the year of the Battle of the Somme, and once again coastal bombardment was used to try to divert as much German effort as possible to coastal defence. By this time the ranks of the monitors had been swelled by the arrival of *Erebus* and *Terror*, the first properly designed 15 inch ships, with enough speed to be practical warships and the ability to hit targets at a range of over 32,000 yards – enough to take on the German shore batteries. The range could be increased even further by heeling the ships. A great effort was made to try to deceive the enemy into thinking that a landing was planned on the Belgian coast, between Ostend and Antwerp. A great bustle of ships, guns and infantry was arranged at all channel ports and 100 trawlers, together with all available monitors and protective destroyers, was assembled and anchored off Dunkirk in full view of the enemy. It remained there for four days, during which the 12 inch and 15 inch ships fired on the coast whenever the weather permitted. For this operation the monitors were protected by a smokescreen which allowed them to get within effective range of the enemy batteries. *Soult* however was hit by a bomb whilst moored in Dunkirk harbour. The damage was not severe but she was docked for repair, whilst at the same time her gun mounts were modified to give them 30 degrees elevation, increasing their range to match that of *Erebus* and *Terror*. General, Sir Douglas Haig, who commanded the Somme Offensive, was moved to write to Bacon commending the help the navy had given in diverting some German forces to defend the channel coast. In reality the effect was probably minimal.

The winter of 1916/17 was extremely cold, making it impossible for the German destroyers to use the Zeebrugge–Bruges Channel, they therefore had to lie alongside the mole at Zeebrugge. Bacon determined to catch them napping there during a spell of especially bad weather, and set off with *Erebus* and *Terror*. The ships had a miserable voyage to a rendezvous off Dunkirk, but the snow got thicker and the weather worse so this promising venture had to be abandoned for lack of visibility.

1917 was a crucial year in the war at sea. Jutland had proved to the Germans that their High Seas Fleet could not find a way to erode the superiority of the Grand Fleet in the North Sea or break the British blockade, so the Imperial Navy did what it should have done from the beginning and concentrated all its efforts on unrestricted submarine warfare. Almost all warship building effort was concentrated on the U-boat fleet. Convinced that this could cut off Britain from supplies and reinforcements from her Allies and her empire, the Germans expected to be able to force her to seek an armistice before the US could come to the aid of the Allies. They were very nearly successful and indeed the Russian revolution and the consequent redeployment of almost a million men from the eastern front to the west, gave the Central Powers real hope of victory. In this context closing the channel to enemy submarine traffic and destroying U-boat facilities on the Belgian coast became a major strategic issue. Monitors were to play a key role in both these efforts.

Early in 1917 Bacon decided to make a determined attempt to use the three 15 inch monitors and whichever of the 12 inch ships was available to do serious damage to the port facilities at Ostend and Zeebrugge. For these operations the sluggard, *Soult* together with *Moore,* one of the 12 inchers, were to be towed, each by one of the new 15 inch ships, so that the convoy, consisting of four large monitors, two small ones, ten destroyers, six paddle minesweepers and a host of motor launches designated to make smoke, could travel at about 10 knots through the water. A constant worry was that *Soult's* 15 inch guns were already showing signs of wear, and no spares were available, as priority was given to the guns of the battleships of the Grand Fleet. There was therefore no question of a sustained bombardment, every round had to tell. The operation was planned to begin on 25 March, but as usual the weather intervened, then there were various accidents and breakdowns so that it did not commence until 11 May, after no less than five false starts. Conditions had to be exactly right, with a light on-shore wind to carry the smoke down onto the batteries and a tide running along the coast so ships at anchor would lie broadside on to the shore line. The primary targets were the lock gates at Zeebrugge and dock facilities at Ostend. Once again visibility was poor on 11 May, so much so that the monitors could not see their aiming mark, *M24,* at the planned 12,000 yards distance, so she had to close to 4,200 yards. This had the effect of seriously reducing the directional accuracy of fire. Accurate fire was important as the lock gates were very small. As Bacon remarked they were only about one tenth the area of the deck of a monitor. On this occasion the monitors were to position themselves around a buoy laid by the destroyer *Lydiard.* To get this accu-

rately in place *Lydiard* had to set off from the South Goodwin
lightship at full speed, drop her buoy after a carefully judged
distance run, and carry straight on until she was almost on
top of the breakwater at Zeebrugge. She then had to turn
round and exactly retrace her course so as to be sure that the
buoy had been correctly positioned. Close to the breakwater
a torpedo was fired at her, but missed. Strangely the navigating officer found the distance recorded on the long leg
from the lightship seemed more accurate than that for the
short run from Zeebrugge. He concluded that this must be
due to the effect of running over shallow water near the
breakwater, and this was taken into account on future
occasions.

The monitors found the buoy in the correct place and
opened fire at 04.45 hours at a range of 26,000 yards. Practice
during the winter had shown that the best way of bringing
the guns quickly onto target in these conditions was to fire
deliberately short at first, making it easier for the spotter
plane to see the bursts and give directional corrections. Then
the range would be steadily increased until hits were
reported. The Germans immediately replied by putting
down a smoke screen, which, fortunately for the British, got
blown in the wrong direction by the light wind. The coastal
guns then opened fire on the monitors so it was the turn of
the British motor launches to lay a smoke screen and this was
successfully carried out. While the monitors were
bombarding the locks another fight was taking place over
their heads. The Royal Navy Air Service had mounted a
major operation to protect the spotting aircraft and to shoot
down enemy spotters and bombers. The British spotter was
successfully protected from some large enemy formations,
but it had unfortunately taken off earlier than necessary and

consequently ran short of petrol after just less than an hour of firing, forcing it to return to Dunkirk. At the same time its relief aircraft broke down and never arrived. For a short time the monitors continued to fire without guidance, but at 06.00 hours the bombardment ceased so as to conserve the precious gun barrels. Bacon had hoped to press on and attack Ostend, but the weather was turning hazy and he did not want to risk his shots falling on the town, so that part of the operation was called off and the ships set off home. This had been an altogether more professional operation than most previous bombardments, and it showed that in spite of the heavy coastal artillery monitors could, in the right conditions, launch an effective attack. Unfortunately however the damage done was not very great. Air reconnaissance in the following days showed plenty of hits within 50-60 yards of the gates but no actual damage to them. Only some sheds and a pump house were hit and these were not critically important. Realistically, as Bacon suspected, the target was too small to expect to hit at such long range. The main lesson learnt was the effectiveness of smoke which had prevented any hits being scored on the attacking ships. Bacon put this down to a new technique for disguising the black cordite smoke made by the monitor's guns with more black smoke made by destroyer's engines as well as the white phosphorous smoke laid by the launches.

On 4 June the weather was fair and reconnaissance had reported a number of ships in Ostend dockyard so *Erebus* and *Terror* set off again, leaving *Soult* and *Moore* behind. They anchored 26,000 yards off shore and opened their bombardment, using the same technique for finding direction and range as they had for the Zeebrugge attack. A spirited action took place. The German batteries replied and the situation became difficult until a Sopwith Pup of the RNAS managed to shoot down the enemy observation balloon. Both sides were using smoke screens, the German one proved more effective than at Zeebrugge, eventually forcing the monitors to cease fire for fear of hitting civilians. One problem encountered was that the ships had started to roll during the course of the barrage, and this tended to upset their aim. The unexpected swell was accounted for by an encounter between British destroyers out of Harwich and some German torpedo boats, the wash of these ships steaming at high speed some 15 miles away had taken half an hour to reach the monitors, but in the calm prevailing conditions and shallow water was still enough to be embarrassing. Nevertheless this proved to be the most successful bombardment so far. A large mine-laying U-boat (*UC.70*) and some other vessels in harbour were destroyed and severe damage done to dock installations. Unfortunately two large floating docks in the basin were not hit. Once again the monitors were unscathed. At last the monitors were benefiting from the years of painful learning of the art of shore bombardment, so that they could begin to contribute substantially to the war effort.

Several more attempts were made that summer, but always something went wrong at the last minute, for example a wind change or a machinery problem. Eventually orders were given that the monitor on guard off Dunkirk should report on conditions three times a day. If the report was favourable, aircraft and smoke-making motor launches would set off immediately and the duty monitor would attack on its own. On the first occasion that this happened *Terror* got into a favourable position but frustratingly the aircraft's radio failed and the replacement machine failed to take over control although it had been ordered to do so. *Terror* could not risk firing without a spotter for fear of hitting civilian targets. On 4 September, *Soult* was able to stagger towards a firing position and, opening up whilst under way, managed to put twenty-eight rounds into dockyard facilities at Ostend but did not damage the vital floating docks. On 22 September however things went much better. This time *Terror* was the duty ship and she severely damaged the dockyard and the floating docks. At the same time the RNAS fighters shot down three enemy seaplanes. This day's operation was a major achievement and it caused the Germans to cease using Ostend as a base for surface vessels. Not to be outdone *Soult* had another go in October, hitting an anti-aircraft ammunition dump and blowing it up.

An amusing event occurred late in September when Bacon took Admirals Jellicoe (First Sea Lord), Oliver (head of naval operations), several other dignitaries together with the American, Admiral Mayo, to see the monitors in action. They were embarked on the destroyer *Broke*. Conditions were not ideal for bombardment but *Terror* was using a searchlight on a small monitor several miles away as an aiming mark, and a spotter plane was over the dockyard at Ostend which the Germans were trying to rebuild after the recent attack. Just as *Broke* drew near her, *Terror*'s great guns trained on the invisible target and she started a steady barrage. The *Tirpitz* battery immediately replied, its shells splashing down very close to *Broke*, in fact they would have almost hit her if she had not by chance altered course a few seconds earlier. Bacon jokingly apologised to the American for altering course and not bringing the hostile fire even nearer, so he could boast at home of having been under fire. "Don't worry about it" the American replied, "by the time I get back to New York and tell the story, I can promise you that that shell will have been

close alongside right enough." Actually that day's bombardment was quite successful, doing substantial damage to the
dockyard.

Terror did not have long to bask in the glory of this achievement. She was lying at anchor outside Dunkirk at about
midnight on 18/19 October when a daring attack was made
by three German torpedo boats, stealing up to her under
cover of darkness and hitting her with three torpedoes then
raking her with gunfire. The torpedoes did serious damage
to the hull, in spite of the bulges, but luckily the watertight
doors had been closed and although there were several feet
of water in the forward compartments, the doors held and
the ship was immediately beached. One of the unsung heroes
of the war at sea, Captain Iron, the harbourmaster from
Dover, was sent for. Iron's father and grandfather had
preceded him in the harbourmaster's post and he was a
consummate expert on all matters relating to salvage. He
arrived early in the morning after the attack with the
powerful salvage tug *Lady Brassey*. He saw that the situation
was serious and summoned a second tug *Lady Crundall,* so
that working together the two were eventually able to
manoeuvre the unwieldy casualty into Dunkirk harbour
where she was beached again. The worst damage had
occurred in the fore part of the ship where the bulge was
narrowest, here much of the hull under water had been
blown away, further aft the bulges had prevented serious
damage. It was impossible to shore up the hull with cement
since repair work was constantly interrupted by air attacks,
but eventually the water was pumped out of most of the
flooded compartments and the bulkheads reinforced so that
Iron decided it was safe to take *Terror* across to Dover, going
slow ahead under her own steam. This went well, but Iron

was concerned about the strain on the bulkheads caused by forward movement and insisted that the passage to Portsmouth, where major repairs could be carried out, must be made stern first to relieve the strain. When she set off however, with Iron on board, Captain Bruton, the commanding officer, refused to follow his advice, and ordered the two tugs, *Lady Brassey* and *Lady Crundall*, to pull her head first. Soon after she set out the weather began to deteriorate and the fore part of the ship became flooded and rode dangerously low in the water. At the same time a powerful salvage pump, which had been shipped in case of emergencies, broke down. The ship wallowed deeper and deeper in the water, eventually becoming impossible to steer and putting a terrific strain on the tow lines. In the early hours of the morning *Terror* was riding to a single line to *Lady Crundall, Brassey*'s hawser having parted, helpless and broadside on to sea. She was impossible to control so Captain Bruton gave the order to abandon ship. Soon after dawn, however, the westerly gale moderated and the crew were re-embarked. The second tow line was once again secured and the two tugs brought the ship back into Dover.

A few days later they tried again. Iron and Bruton were still at loggerheads and although the ship left Dover stern first, Bruton soon gave the order to turn her round. This was too much for Iron and he ordered one of the tugs to come alongside and take him off; he wanted nothing to do with the shipwreck which he expected to result from Bruton's ridiculous manoeuvre. At this Bruton changed his mind and decided to continue stern first after all. In this condition the ship reached Portsmouth safely and only turned round to enter harbour bow first when she was well inside the Solent. This was an unfortunate example of the

arrogance of a typical naval officer of the period, and of
the contempt with which the Royal Navy often regarded
civilian expertise.

Unfortunately *Erebus* was put out of action shortly afterwards. On 28 October she was steaming about 20 miles off
Ostend when she was attacked in an alarmingly novel way.
The Germans had been experimenting with high speed
remotely controlled motor boats. These were 43 feet long and
could make about 30 knots, they contained 1,450lb of high
explosive, enough to do serious damage to a big ship. They
were powered by two petrol engines, which the crew would
start up in harbour. They would then take the boat a few
miles out to sea. The crew would then leave the boat and
hand over control to a remote operator ashore. He steered the
boat with an electrically operated rudder actuated by means
of 30 miles of cable paid out astern of the boat. The operator
was given instructions by a seaplane acting as spotter. The
British had seen these advanced weapons on several
occasions, once when one went out of control and crashed
into a dockyard wall, and another time when a determined
attack was made on the small monitor *M23*, which managed
to destroy the attacker using her 3 inch close range quick
firers. *Erebus* was not so lucky, suffering the effects of the only
successful attack made by these fearsome craft. Despite a hail
of fire from her own close range armament and from the
supporting destroyers, the remotely controlled boat was seen
to cut across her stern, turn through 180 degrees and smash
into her bulge amidships. There was a terrific explosion and
debris was hurled far and wide, killing two men
and wounding fifteen others. Luckily the bulge had absorbed
most of the impact. *Erebus* returned under her own steam to
Dover, then on to Portsmouth for further repairs. It was

found that there was a 50 foot long tear in the outer bulge and some minor structural damage to the hull. She was quickly back in service. Remote controlled motor boats made at least one further attack, this time on the destroyer *North Star*, which sunk the attacker with gunfire, they then seem to have been abandoned. The remotely controlled boats were not considered to be a serious threat to ships because although the boats themselves were low in the water and difficult to see, they set up such a wash that any alert watch keeper would spot them and give the gun crews some target practice.

These two attacks on the newest and most formidable of the monitors did demonstrate very clearly how excellent their underwater protection was. Similar strikes on even a super dreadnought battleship might well have proved fatal, *Audacious*, for example, had been sunk by a single mine filled with less than 200 lbs of explosive.

Apart from coastal bombardment, guard duties and net patrol, the Dover Patrol had two more ambitious projects which would involve the monitors. The first was a scheme for landing in force at Ostend, during which a force of soldiers and marines would seize the port and its perimeter, knock out the heavy guns in the batteries, and hold the town until French and Belgian forces could move up the coast to link up with the beachhead. Bacon's plan for this was nothing if not ambitious. He argued that seizing Ostend would severely hamper enemy U-boat operations and incline the Dutch to take the Allies' side, as well as enabling the Allied armies on the left flank of the line in France to threaten severely the whole German position in northern France. The scheme was to load a force of 10,000 men into ninety trawlers (100 men each!) and six 12 inch and three 9.2 inch monitors.

These forces would be made ready in the greatest secrecy and
would approach the coast so as to arrive at dawn. Their
approach would be covered by smoke boats, towed by
ancient merchant ships, protecting the monitors and trawlers
from enemy fire. The 12 inch monitors would try to silence
the heavy enemy guns while the quick firers would create
havoc on the waterfront and around the harbour. The monitors and the trawlers would go right alongside the jetties to
unload their troops, and the monitors would remain alongside to act as a magazine for the troops, providing heavy
artillery support when needed. They would be carrying
between them twenty-two armoured cars, sixteen tanks,
motorised machine gun units and field guns as well as troops
and ammunition. The trawlers, having discharged their
troops, would sweep mines in the harbour approach and in
the harbour itself, so that eventually transport ships could
land supplies and reinforcements. The small monitors would
prevent submarines and any other hostile ships from leaving
the harbour and if necessary moor so as to provide a bridge
for the invaders between various parts of the town and port.
A vital task for the ground forces would be to seize the lock
gates so that they could flood low lying land at will, cutting
off and starving out enemy troops in outlying batteries. As
soon as the beachhead was secure and the heavy guns
silenced, further troops, ferried in channel steamers, would
be called up and would enter the harbour, then strike down
south westwards towards Ypres, taking the German Army in
the rear.

Secrecy and surprise were the key elements of the whole
plan. Troops were not to be briefed until just before
embarking. Dover was to be cut off from the world during
embarkation, diversions were planned with the big monitors

making a sustained attack on Westende, and enemy intelligence was to be misled whenever possible. Special arrangements were planned for laying nets to keep the area clear of U-boats. Bacon was worried that the enemy might have laid electrically detonated ground mines in the harbour and its approaches, so a submarine was delegated to search the bottom for control wires, grapple them and cut them.

   In the end the whole scheme came to nothing. Although both French and Haig, successive commanders of the British forces in France, were interested in the idea, neither was prepared to commit the army to making the advances in Flanders which formed an integral part of the plan. Also it seemed unlikely that the amphibious landing would be able to clear Ostend of enemy forces before reinforcements arrived from Germany. The generals pointed out that experience indicated that while fire from the ship's heavy guns could flatten the buildings of the town, this in fact made the streets easier to defend than if they were left standing, since piles of rubble and shell craters made excellent defensive positions, and in any case the 10,000 troops allocated would not be enough to seize the town by street fighting. Probably the soldier's judgement was correct. A seaborne landing on a strongly occupied enemy coast, defended, as Ostend was, by heavy artillery batteries, is an extremely difficult undertaking even for the most skilled and best trained troops. The troops allocated for the proposed assault would have had no specialist training, and would probably have been raw recruits. Secrecy prevented any rehearsals even for officers. Communications between the ships and forward units on land, vital for directing gunfire, would have been most difficult to maintain. Also the German Army during the war proved itself to be skilled and stubborn in defence, quick to respond to emergencies and able to mount rapid and effective counter attacks. Good railway connections between Ostend and Germany would have made it easy to rush in reinforcements, including artillery. The other doubtful element was the weather. Exactly the right wind and sea conditions would have been essential to make the plan for bringing the monitors up to the jetties, protected by smoke, at all viable. It is easy to imagine chaos resulting from changes of plan brought about by unforeseen weather or tidal conditions. The reason given by Bacon for the abandonment of the project was the erection of a new German battery at Knocke, which could fire directly on the jetties at Ostend, but in reality it was a hare brained scheme from the start and did not have the support of the army.

Bacon, however, was not a man to be deterred from his object of taking the battle to the enemy. He felt strongly that German forces must be forcibly expelled from the Belgian coast before any kind of truce or armistice could be contemplated. (There were several straws in the wind suggesting the possibility of an armistice in 1917). If the enemy troops remained in Belgium he foresaw the eventual domination of Holland and Denmark by Germany so that the whole continental coast of the North Sea would be in German hands (as indeed it was between 1940 and 1945). He also thought, correctly, that the Belgian ports put Germany in a perfect position to raid British commerce passing through the Dover Strait or into the Thames and that someday the Germans would wake up to the strength of their hand in this regard and use their destroyers and cruisers to add to the havoc already being created by their U-boats. Bacon's ideas in fact fitted in well with military strategy then in vogue. The Americans had as yet played no substantial part in the war, and would not be in a position to do so for eighteen months at least. The French army was close to mutiny, their troops would in no circumstances attack and could only with difficulty be cajoled into continuing to fight at all. Britain was within a few weeks of running out of food due to the activities of the U-boats. Jellicoe, the First Sea Lord, was extremely concerned about the danger of the enemy gaining the upper hand in the southern North Sea; he wrote "We are carrying on the war as if we had absolute command of the sea. We have not . . . Our present policy is heading straight for disaster".

Together with Haig, Bacon planned an initiative in Flanders which would enable the British Army to strike up from its positions near Ypres and meet up with an amphibious landing in force on the Belgian coast, not in a town this time, but on an open beach. To achieve this vital junction the army in Flanders would have to advance about 20 miles which Haig believed was then quite feasible. Scarcely had the Ostend project been abandoned then serious planning for what was to be called "The Great Landing" got well under way.

Once again this plan was predicated on co-ordinating a raid on the coast with a rapid advance on land which would meet up with the seaborne forces. This time, however, instead of landing by seizing a heavily defended harbour, the attack would be made on an open beach between Nieuwport and Ostend. This would put an Allied division east of the flooded area of Flanders endangering the whole right flank of the German Army.

The shore in the area consisted of a tidal beach rising to a sea wall 30 feet high and sloping at an angle of 30 degrees. At the top of the wall, semi-circular coping stones overhung the slope and formed an obstacle. The sea wall was defended by small arms and machine guns. Obviously landing parties would have to have effective covering fire and have some means of scaling the wall, but the water offshore was shallow, shelving gently, with sand bars covering at high water, making it impossible to approach with any sort of conventional sea going troop carrying vessel. The terrible losses accompanying the Gallipoli landings showed that using small boats to ferry troops from troopers offshore to an enemy held beach was to invite 20-30 per cent casualties in the invading forces before they even got to land. Monitors with their heavy armament and shallow draft seemed to provide a possible solution. Not only that but the 12 inch monitors were considered to be readily expendable. Their guns had a range of only just over half that of the coastal batteries so they were of limited use for coastal bombardment. Their main employment was as guard ships for nets and harbours such as Dunkirk and those duties could be adequately performed by small monitors. They were far too slow to be any use to the Grand Fleet. Perhaps, however, their size, shallow draft and powerful guns could provide the key to a successful landing.

Bacon set about the problem with his usual enthusiasm and flair for innovation. His first idea was to build long troop carrying barges alongside which two monitors would be secured, so that they could push the shallow draft barges close to the beach. This would be done at high tide to minimise the height difference between the landing forces and the top of the sea wall. To test the feasibility of this system he had a very careful study made of the topography of the beaches and of the sea wall. This was done by using aircraft to photograph the beach regularly every hour as the tide rose and fell. At the same time a submarine was sent to sit on the bottom as close to the shore as it could get and take regular measurements of the depth of water above it. From these two sets of data an accurate picture could be built up of the shape of the beach and its adjacent waters, and show how they could be approached at high tide. So as not to give the enemy a clue as to what was afoot, photographs were taken all along the coastline, but the only ones which interested Bacon were of about 2 miles of coast between Westende and Middlekirke. Here it was that the landing would take place.

The results of the survey showed that the monitors would ground some 300 yards offshore, so to get the troops ashore dry shod the barges would have to be at least 300 yards long. This simply wasn't practical. The question then arose as to whether the monitors could push the barges from behind. This would mean that the length of the barges required could be reduced by the length of the monitor (112 yards). The beam of the barges should be roughly 20 feet, so that they would fit snugly between the bows of two pushing monitors (see picture 8 and drawing 10). A length of 200 yards was chosen for the barges. The "pontoons" as Bacon called the barges, could have a draft of roughly 9 feet at the seaward end where the monitors would be pushing, and 18 inches at the landward end from which the troops would disembark. So as to be able to disembark vehicles, tanks and artillery, a very shallow draft timber raft supported by barrels to give to buoyancy would be secured in front of each of the barges and this was designed to run right up onto the beach. To enable it to support heavy weights, stout wooden legs could be put down beneath the raft as soon as it beached. Charles Lillicrap, the original designer of the monitors, was drafted in to design the barges, he suggested that as the 12 inch monitors only needed half their engine power to get up to 6 knots, two of them using their full power should be able to push these extraordinary contraptions at about that speed. The first barge was quickly built on the Thames and tested. There was at first some difficulty in lashing the barge securely to the monitors, but eventually, using heavy chains in place of the original cables, this problem was overcome and Bacon was delighted to find that the barges could indeed be pushed at about 6 knots and that by using full rudder and reversing engines when necessary, it was possible to steer the extraordinary contrivance.

As soon as the successful test had taken place the Great Landing became a priority activity for the Dover Patrol. Three landing spots, "Hopital", "2nd Maison Isolee", and "Fan" were selected with two alternatives, "Casino" and "Blue Terrain". These were all spots which seemed from the aerial photographs to have suitable beach contours. Getting the slow, clumsy vessels into exactly the right place was a further challenge. The tide runs strongly along the shoreline, especially at high water so there was every possibility of a fatal navigational error. To deal with this, large leading marks were erected off Dunkirk, which the ships would keep in line so as to ensure that they were steering the correct course. To measure distance run along this course correctly, two coastal motor boats would travel just ahead of the monitors, paying out a long wire, one end of which was anchored in a known position close to the leading marks. When the motor boats had paid out the length of wire which showed they had reached the spot where the monitors should turn in towards the beach, they would drop a lighted buoy to act as a turning mark. In trials in the Thames Estuary this turned out to be an extremely accurate means of navigation.

During the whole period leading up to the operation the ship's crews were placed in strict quarantine with no contact whatever with the shore. All letters were strictly censored and even a special hospital ship was provided so that anyone falling sick would not have to be taken ashore, leading to the danger of a possible breach of security. Even this was not enough to satisfy Bacon's enthusiasm for secrecy. The crews were specifically told that they were practicing for a landing east of Zeebrugge, not near Westende.

The problem still remained of getting the troops and vehicles across the sea wall and storming the defences on the other side. For this it was decided that as well as extra quick firers and pom poms on the barges, three tanks should be carried on each barge, two of them "male" tanks with two 6 pounder guns and one "female" with multiple machine guns. The question remained of how to get the tanks over the sea wall, which was too steep for them to climb. After a lot of experiments, involving building a replica sea wall at the tank HQ in France, a wedge shaped wooden structure was devised which would be pushed against the sea wall and provide a gently sloping ramp for the tanks to climb. As well as the fire from the tanks and light weapons, the 12 inch guns of the monitors would clear the way for the assault troops. The support of four of these massive guns for each of the three rafts would be extremely welcome during the landing, however firing them over the heads of the soldiers in the barges would result in all of them being deafened and perhaps more seriously injured by the blast and shock. Special low power, close range, propellant charges were therefore provided.

Between them the three barges would contain about 13,500 officers and men, with all their equipment including motor cycles, cars, ambulances, cycles and divisional field artillery.

The landing was to take place at dawn and should come as a complete surprise to the enemy. To cover the assault from the heavy coastal guns, smoke generators were mounted on the monitors and smoke would also be made by the accompanying motor boats and destroyers. At the same time the three usable 15 inch monitors, *Soult, Erebus* and *Terror* would commence a heavy bombardment further east, around Ostend, to try to divert the enemy's attention and to make it difficult to move reinforcements towards the landing. Bacon was perhaps unduly optimistic about smoke. There were only a few days in each month when the tide would be right for the landing, and smoke would be ineffective if the wind was in the wrong direction, therefore the expedition would have to trust to luck as regards the weather on the critical day.

The procedure for launching the attack was carefully planned. Four days before the landing day, in the dark, the monitors and barges would emerge from the Swin, where they were moored, the barges under tow from the monitors. The barges would be anchored in the Downs, where any German aircraft would take them for some sort of protection for the shipping there, while the monitors went on the Dover to refuel. They would take the minimum possible fuel load to minimise draft for the operation. The following night the monitors would return to collect the barges and take them to Dunkirk, tugs would moor them inside the harbour where they would stay during the daylight hours, with the monitors alongside to hide them from view. Enhanced air patrols would keep away enemy observers. Two nights were allocated for loading the barges. When this was complete the men would be taken aboard the monitors and as soon as it was dark monitors and barges would move out and be secured to buoys outside the harbour. When it was time to move off, the monitors would be lashed together then move up to the barges. The chains would be secured and the convoy, consisting of the six 12 inch monitors with barges, motor boats, trawlers, destroyers and small monitors, who would give extra fire support, would move off. The 15 inch monitors would already be getting ready to open their diversionary barrage. At the appointed place the motor boats would drop their lighted buoys and the monitor/barge combinations would turn towards the shore as they reached them, keeping their bows pointing slightly to port to counteract the tide running westward along the coast. The troops would move from the monitors onto the barges. Five minutes before they ran on the shore smoke would be released and the small monitors would open fire. Just before the rafts ran ashore the 12 inch guns of the large monitors would open up on the coastal defences. The tanks would waddle ashore followed by the infantry and together they would probe inland and fan out along the shore, capturing, if possible, the enemy gun positions at Westende. They would form a defensive perimeter then thrust down towards friendly forces advancing from Ypres. The 12 inch monitors would withdraw, whilst the newly landed division, together with the advancing army from Ypres, would re-occupy the Belgian coast and isolate the right wing of the German Army. German communications would be in chaos because the advancing army would have overrun the vital railway junction at Rouliers, the key to rail communication in western Flanders. There was even a scheme to transport 18 inch guns across from England, lashed to the bulges of monitors, and install them in the Palace Hotel at Westende, where they would be used to destroy the docks and locks at Zeebrugge

Tremendous effort and thought had been invested in the plan, but it never materialised. The British push forward from Ypres towards the Passchendaele Ridge made some progress but it was painfully slow, and achieved at terrible cost. Twice the normal level of rainfall, together with the destruction of the drainage system by shell fire left the battle-field a sea of filthy sucking mud which drowned horses, men, guns and even tanks. By early October it was clear that the army on land was going to get nowhere near achieving its objectives and on the 15th the forces designated for the amphibious operation were stood down. Bacon argued vociferously for a reduced scheme which would simply establish a beachhead and hold it without any expectation of a junction, with forces moving up from Ypres, but the idea was rejected by the army. He was bitterly disappointed that yet another of his aggressive schemes had been frustrated.

Would there have been a possibility of success if the scheme had gone ahead? It certainly depended on a lot of complex co-ordination of a large force, at night, under the heavy guns of the enemy. Thousands of things could have gone wrong, a change of wind, tanks refusing to start, prema-ture discovery of the operation by a German patrol – the list is almost endless – but military experts at the time did not judge it to be completely impractical. As Bacon argued the potential gain was huge and the cost, even if all six monitors were lost and most of the soldiers killed or made prisoner, was affordable in the horrific context of the world war. Bacon's reduced scheme for an unsupported landing however would almost certainly have led to disaster. Re-supply of the force would have been difficult and costly and with the railway system intact the Germans could easily have moved up troops and heavy guns to pin the landing down and drive the invaders back into the sea. Experience in the Second World War was to show how difficult landings on an occupied coast can be and how overwhelming superiority on land, at sea and in the air is essential to achieve success. In the light of experiences such as the Dieppe Raid it is probably a mercy that Bacon's schemes came to nothing.

Bacon had one more plan involving bringing the monitors into action on the enemy coast. This was what was eventually to turn into the famous Zeebrugge Raid of 1918. Bacon's scheme was very different to the one that was actually carried out, in which a cruiser was used instead of three monitors, however the ultimate object of both was to prevent submarines based at Bruges from going to sea via the port at Zeebrugge. Bacon's plan was to build a false bow onto a 12 inch monitor and also provide it with an angled rotatable gangway on its bows. The monitor would be rammed into the seaward side of the mole, collapsing the false bow and allowing the soldiers on board to swarm along the gangway, over the parapet of the mole, and onto the inshore side of it. Here their first job would be to blow up any ships alongside the mole (there were normally two or three destroyers). They would then destroy machinery and stores in the harbour area. In the meantime two other monitors would anchor very close to the mole and shell the lock gates at very close range (about 2,000 yards). From such a position they could hardly miss. Once the gates were destroyed the soldiers would re-embark and the monitors would steam away. While all this was going on blockships would steam into the harbour and sink themselves so as to make assurance double sure. Once again smoke would be used to protect the attackers, and a diversionary bombardment made on the coastal guns at Knoke. Had this plan been successful it would have had a major impact on the submarine war, as a large part of the U-boat force would have been bottled up in Bruges. The scheme which replaced it and was eventually carried out, by Bacon's successor was executed with great skill and daring, but was almost useless as the lock gates were not bombarded and the blockship sunk in the harbour was so positioned that, after a little work with a dredger, the U-boats were able to squeeze round the obstruction. Bacon's plan would have been far more effective, but it was blocked by the Admiralty because they did not believe that it would be possible to bring the monitors into position alongside the mole in view of the fierce tide which set past it and the proximity of the enemy batteries. Bacon argued until his dying day that the monitors could have managed it.

By December 1917 however Bacon's star was beginning to wane. "The Streaky One", as he was called by those who disliked him, had displayed woeful lack of tact when dealing with the Admiralty and was secretive, arrogant and stubborn. In particular he had made dangerous enemies in the anti-submarine committee formed by the Admiralty and led by the formidable Admiral Roger Keyes. Bacon refused to follow any of the committee's advice about building an effective anti-submarine barrier across the channel, and also ignored its recommendation that he should allow patrolling warships to use their searchlights when patrolling nets at night. The battle between Keyes and Bacon became bitter and personal. While Jellicoe was First Sea Lord, Bacon's position remained just sustainable, but when he was replaced by Admiral, Sir Rosslyn Wemyss, late in 1917, the tables were turned, Bacon was sacked and replaced by Keyes himself.

At first there was little change in policy as regards the monitors, except that the small ships were on patrol more often, using their searchlights to try to force submarines to dive and consequently run afoul of the deep minefields being laid to trap them. Keyes wanted to change the practice as far as coastal bombardment was concerned by encouraging the 15 inch ships to make rapid hit and run (insofar as the word "run" can be applied to monitors) attacks whenever conditions were favourable. This had been the practice eventually developed by Keyes during the Gallipoli campaign, and he considered the carefully prepared bombardments which Bacon had carried out to be unduly complex. In particular he believed that aerial observation took too long to set up and organise, and another system for aiming must be developed. To achieve this he devoted almost two months to making an accurate map of the Belgian coast, including all known gun positions, watch towers and searchlights. This had to be done by surveying officers working in small boats protected from enemy interference by destroyers and by the monitors themselves. By the end of February an accurate map had been made and superimposed on the charts. At the same time the Altham gyro director was coming into use, this device made it much easier for guns to be aimed at an unseen target, so that if a ship knew its own position it could fire "blind" with a reasonable chance of being correctly aligned. The new method came into use but was not, as we shall see, notably successful.

An unfortunate incident took place on 15 February. The 12 inch monitors which normally protected the fishing vessels patrolling the anti-submarine nets between Dieppe and Folkestone were all under repair and only a single small monitor, *M26*, together with some destroyers, was guarding the net patrol in the channel. With her big guns the monitor was supposed be able to see off any enemy torpedo boats or destroyers. The Germans had chosen this very night to make a strong destroyer raid on the nets and on their defenders, so as to cover the passage through the nets of a group of submarines. The result was a disaster. The enemy destroyers went unchallenged so that a trawler and seven drifters were sunk, and a paddle minesweeper was badly damaged. *M26* and her supporting destroyers seemed to have hung around doing nothing at all in spite of gunfire and flares all round them. They actually saw the German destroyers making their escape but assumed they must be British. This was especially serious because the civilian fisherman crews of the trawler and drifters felt the navy had deserted them. The captain of *M26*, Commander Mellin, was hauled over the coals and dismissed his command, but a court marshal exonerated him of charges of negligence. Keyes was furious.

Terror was the first to make use of the new arrangement for "ad hoc" bombardment. She and *M25* had been moored off Dunkirk when nine enemy destroyers supported by torpedo boats appeared out of the darkness and opened fire. *Terror* fired star shell while British and French destroyers in the offing engaged the invaders. They turned round and fled back to Ostend, two of their torpedo boats being sunk and one destroyer damaged. Unfortunately the British destroyer *Botha* was torpedoed and damaged by one of the French ships. It was clear that the enemy destroyers had taken cover in Ostend harbour and *Terror* with some supporting small ships set off to try to destroy them there. At first she fired at a range of 26,500 yards by dead reckoning, then an aircraft arrived and spotted for her. Enemy guns from the Deutschland battery returned her fire, dropping 15 inch shells all round her but failing to score a hit. They were working at maximum range and the shells were plunging steeply downwards as they entered the water. A smoke screen was deployed and the British bombardment continued until enemy smoke obscured the target completely so that Keyes, in a destroyer, was afraid that his shells might be falling on Belgian civilians. In all thirty-nine 15 inch rounds had been fired and extensive damage done to the dockyard but the destroyers appeared to have moved off.

The Zeebrugge Raid (23 April 1918) was the one assault from the sea which did eventually go ahead, in spite of several postponements as result of bad weather. In it the monitors played a relatively minor part, acting as covering forces and firing on enemy batteries so as to keep them occupied. The Germans had by this time developed a system of direction and distance finding by acoustic means and the return fire from their batteries often came unpleasantly close to the ships very rapidly, however there were no direct hits except for two aerial bombs which struck *Erebus* doing only minor damage. Keyes's policy of hit and run raids however continued, and he seems to have been more willing than Bacon to risk allowing the 12 inch ships to fire from inside the range of the shore batteries. New techniques developed for generating smoke screens laid by coastal motor boats enabled far more activity to be carried out in reasonable safety within the range of enemy guns.

Even the net patrols were not always without incident in 1918. On one occasion, in May 1918, *Terror* was patrolling mined nets off the Belgian coast when her escorting destroyers, led by the powerful new destroyer leader *Termagant*, started signalling to each other and then dashed off towards the Belgian coast. Captain Bruton of the *Terror* flashed an immediate recall but the destroyers, like excited terriers, disregarded all signals and continued their charge, which had been prompted by one of the patrol seeing a force of German destroyers steaming out of Zeebrugge. The sea was rough and a vigorous exchange of gunfire between the rival destroyers produced no result, so a few hours later *Termagant* returned to her boring escort duties and her captain faced a severe dressing down by Bruton, the senior officer present. Why had he ignored six recall signals? Why had he dashed off without orders? The affair was taken to the commodore in charge of the Dunkirk squadron with Bruton pressing for disciplinary action to be taken. *Termagant's* captain however was none other than Andrew Cunningham, who we shall meet as commander-in-chief Mediterranean in the Second World War. He swore, almost certainly untruthfully, that he had not seen the recall signal and as he was a promising officer, full of the aggressive spirit that Keyes admired, the affair was forgotten.

The summer of 1918 saw two interesting developments in the monitor fleet. The first was the mounting of enormous 18 inch guns on the after deck of the 12 inch ships *Wolfe* and *Clive*. These great guns, the largest ever fitted to British warships, had been built for a new generation of battle cruisers, which were rapidly re-designed as aircraft carriers, making their turrets redundant. Two of the massive weapons were delivered to the army in France, and the other two found their way onto the monitors with the idea that they might enable a more effective long range bombardment of Zeebrugge. The 18 inch turret was so large, although it had only one gun, that it could only be trained to starboard and rotated through about 15 degrees. This meant that the ship had to lie starboard side on to her target, and achieve coarse training of the gun by using two anchors and trimming the anchor chains. Firing the guns, whose projectile weighed about one and a half tons, and travelled at 2,270 ft/sec, drove the ship sideways and made her roll violently from side to side, making aiming difficult. The recoil also tended to cause the anchors to drag. The other significant event was the arrival of *Gorgon*, sister ship to the unfortunate *Glatton*. The very long range of her guns was to make her an important asset. Her long range high trajectory fire must have reminded anyone with an interest in naval history of the "bomb ketches" of old.

Gorgon got into action first, firing on German shore batteries at 33,000 yards, accompanied by *Soult*, continuing Keyes's aggressive hit and run tactic. Developments on land were by now moving apace and it seemed that the stalemate which had prevailed since 1914 was coming to an end. First a determined assault from the Germans threatened to drive a wedge between British and French forces in Northern France. Specially trained and equipped German assault troops smashed their way through the Allied lines, driving all before them. There was a real threat to the whole Allied position in France and this could only be countered by a general withdrawal and the abandonment of the ports of Dunkirk and Calais. It takes little imagination to realise what a traumatic event this would be for the war at sea. The Royal Navy hurriedly made plans for colossal minefields all along the French coast and the redeployment of elements of the Grand Fleet, now reinforced by American battleships, to the channel. Luckily all this proved to be unnecessary. The German advance faltered when the troops got too far ahead of their railheads and their artillery cover, and it fizzled out altogether when it encountered stiff resistance from British and Commonwealth forces supported by heavy guns and numerous tanks. The scene was set for the great British counter attack which was to be one of the most impressive military achievements of the war.

While the German advance took place the Royal Navy had been forced to suspend most of its aggressive activity along the Belgian coast, waiting to see if it might be urgently needed to attempt to defend the channel ports, but as the Germans, demoralised, short of food and ammunition and longing to be home, started to stream back towards their own borders, there came a fine opportunity to harass them further. On 27 September no less than seven large monitor, *Erebus, Terror, Gorgon, Eugene, Moore, Crauford* and the 18 inch *Wolfe* set off from Dunkirk. The operation was a diversionary night time attack on Ostend and Zeebrugge to try to bluff the enemy into thinking that a repeat of the Zeebrugge Raid was in the offing. At one stage even one of the barges made for the "Great Landing" that never happened was towed over to add to the deception. The ships then moved westwards to attack communication lines ashore. *Wolfe* opened fire at 36,000 yards with her 18 inch gun, this being the first time such a weapon was used effectively at sea. (The only other ships ever fitted with 18 inch guns were the spectacularly unsuccessful Japanese *Yamato* class battleships). *Wolfe's* target was a railway bridge at Snaeskerke, 3 miles inland from Ostend. *Wolfe* was supported by a small monitor acting as an aiming mark to seaward to give directional orientation and her director tower had to pass aiming instructions not only to the gun turrets but also to the capstans controlling the fore and aft anchor chains which gave coarse direction to the gun. She needed the assistance of tugs to keep her in place as her stern anchor persisted in dragging and the whole ship tried to skid sideways due to the recoil from the great gun. She achieved quite good accuracy, but the bridge was not destroyed although she used up almost all of her eighty rounds of ammunition. *Wolfe* was joined by *Clive* a few days later, but spotting conditions were poor and not many rounds were expended before fire had to be suspended as Allied troops were advancing close behind the retreating Germans. *Gorgon* was firing at the same target and actually hit the bridge, although it was not completely destroyed. Meanwhile the other monitors fired on the coastal batteries, *Moore* achieving a direct hit on a coastal ammunition dump.

The exercise was repeated on 14 October, except that *Gorgon* was assigned the Middlekirke batteries as her target. Having strafed these she moved up the coast at 16 knots, accompanying Keyes in a destroyer, firing at any convenient coastal target. *Eugene* and *Moore* struggled along behind them at their best speed, about 6.5 knots. To the west the shore batteries seemed to be losing heart, or to have been evacuated, but further east *Gorgon* and the destroyers suddenly ran into a very heavy barrage and had to retire at full speed, *Gorgon* surprising her attackers by replying with her after guns, a feat which other monitors could not perform. *Gorgon* was not hit and returned the next day to have a final go at the Snaeskerke Bridge. Hers were the last rounds fired by the monitors during the war. A reconnaissance of the shore batteries during the next few days found them deserted and the guns gone. Keyes himself landed, accompanied by the king of the Belgians to liberate Ostend. This was nearly the end of him as he made the mistake of setting out in a small dinghy into a rough sea and only just escaped being swamped. A boat put out to help him was not so lucky and sunk with loss of life. During the same night (20 Sept 1918), less than a mile away, *M21* struck a shallow mine and was sunk. A sad ending for a ship which had survived four years of tough and dangerous patrolling.

What had the monitors contributed to the war effort? It is difficult in the Twenty-First Century to imagine the attitude to the Royal Navy which prevailed before 1914. "We want eight and we won't wait" was the slogan promoted by the *Daily Mail*, referring to the number of dreadnoughts the newspaper wanted the government to build and it became widely popular. In those days it was not social security, health, transport, or housing that people wanted their tax money spent on. It was the navy. It would bring Britain glory and riches as it had years ago. It would win a new Trafalgar against anyone who dared to challenge it. How disappointing then that as soon as war broke out, all the Grand Fleet could do was to hide itself from enemy submarines in obscure northern sea lochs. There was no new Trafalgar, and the only clash with the enemy fleet, at Jutland, resulted in a disappointing inconclusive stalemate.

In fact the posture adopted by the Grand Fleet was the sound strategy, leading to the eventual starvation and surrender of the enemy. Naval men however were sorely disappointed by the situation. As their ships swung to their moorings in Scapa Flow they thought uncomfortably about their brothers and friends fighting bayonet to bayonet or hand to hand in France and dying in their thousands. At least one officer elected to salve his conscience by spending his leave fighting as a soldier in the trenches.

Of course not all of the navy was inactive. The small ships of the Dover Patrol and the Harwich Force of destroyers and light cruisers were busy at sea, chasing enemy torpedo boats and submarines. In support of them were the trawlers, drifters and minesweepers, manned largely by volunteers from the Royal Naval Volunteer Reserve and the Royal Naval Minesweeping Reserve, and the host of small, armed, ships which enforced the blockade of Germany. This was dangerous work, performed with daring and skill but it was not glamorous, and much of it was essentially defensive. Where was the proud, aggressive Royal Navy which people had so patriotically supported in the peacetime years?

It was this sense of inadequacy which led to the madcap schemes for invading northern Germany which the monitors were designed to lead. When these ventures were abandoned they were replaced by the ill-planned Dardanelles campaign in which monitors played no decisive part. The sustained bombardments of the Belgian coast by the massive guns of the later monitors and the preparations for amphibious landings may have done something to assuage the guilty feeling of senior naval officers, frustrated by the supine attitude of the Grand Fleet, but they didn't worry the enemy much. The Germans had to garrison the Belgian coast using men and guns which would have been useful elsewhere, but in the big scheme of things this was no more than a minor embarrassment. Even the Zeebrugge Raid only resulted in a handful of casualties on the German side, and represented a poor return for all the planning and effort put into the various schemes for coastal raids. If the monitors were supposed to be the aggressive arm of British sea power, that arm was a miniscule one.

One action, by itself however, justified the existence of the monitor force. There can be no doubt that the cheap unseaworthy ex-Brazilian gunboats played a crucial part checking the German advance along the Belgian coast in 1914. If this had continued and Dunkirk and Calais had been lost, how could

France have been saved from a disaster like that of 1870? No other ships could have managed the sustained close range bombardment achieved by *Humber, Mersey* and *Severn* during those crucial few days in 1914. In the following years the later monitors assumed another equally vital role. As guardships at Calais and Dunkirk and watchers over the various anti-submarine obstacles in the Channel they certainly thwarted German schemes to use their Belgium based destroyer force to challenge the British domination of the Dover Strait. In the defence of narrow waters of the Channel, where their gun power made up for their lack of speed, the plodding monitors played a vital, if tedious, part. Only rarely did German ships venture near their formidable armament and they invariably fled when the monitors opened fire. This defensive role was vital to keeping open the lifeline between England and France. It was not glamorous, it was uncomfortable and boring in the extreme, but it was vital to the prosecution of the war.

Financial calculations can be a poor guide to strategy but in this case they are worth consideration. The total cost of the monitor force was roughly as follows:

Class	No built	Cost each (£k)	Total cost
14"	4	550*	2,200
12"	8	215	1,720
First 15"	2	270	540
Second 15"	2	380	760
Ex Brazilian	3	155	465
Ex Norwegian	2	370	740
Small Monitors	19	35	665
Total			£7,090k

*Includes main armament bought new from Bethlehem Steel, all other ships except the ex Brazilians and ex Norwegians used redun-

dant items from obsolete warships, the cost of these second hand turrets is not included.

The total cost of these forty ships was thus a little less than the cost of two battleships (a battleship. at the time cost about £4M) It would be difficult to argue that an extra dreadnaught or two swinging at moorings in Scapa Flow, would have contributed as much to the prosecution of the war at sea as did the monitors. The money could of course have been usefully spent on destroyers which cost an average of roughly £250,000 each, so the monitor fleet would have been equivalent in value to about twenty-eight extra destroyers. These would certainly have been a welcome addition to the navy's strength but a comparatively small one. Britain started the war with 240 destroyers and built 294 during the war. Seventy were lost during the conflict. Had destroyers been built in place of the monitors therefore, the impact on the total strength of the destroyer force would have been marginal, increasing numbers by only about five per cent. On this basis it seems that the monitor fleet gave pretty good value for money.

It is also important to recognise that the enemy was faced by a new and unexpected challenge in the shape of the monitors. This gave Britain a useful surprise factor especially in the actions against enemy raiders in the Channel and in the actions in the Gulf of Trieste and in East Africa. They were a new and unexpected element injected into the war at sea and as such offered the Royal Navy a significant advantage to which the Germans had no easy answer. Their apparent invulnerability to torpedoes and ability to survive mine strikes must have been especially frustrating to submarines and minelayers alike.

The cost of the various classes of monitor also shows

clearly what astonishingly good value for money the smaller unnamed ships offered. We have already seen what a vital contribution the river gunboats made to the defence of France in October 1914 and the excellent work done by the small monitors in the Channel and in the Dardanelles. As the table shows their cost was miniscule when set against their achievements.

As well as offering good value, the clumsy, slow, lightly armoured monitors proved surprisingly durable. Only one of the big ships (*Raglan*) was lost during the war. Of the small monitors only *M15*, *M21*, *M28* and *M30* fell victims to enemy action, not a bad record for a class of ships exposed to more risks than almost any other and designed to be "expendable". One other ship (*Glatton*) blew up by accident. Comparison to the destroyer fleet is interesting:

	Total used	Losses	Loss %
Monitors	40	6	15
Destroyers	534	70	13.1

Chapter 6

After the Armistice

T he Armistice did not mark the end of the fighting for the monitor fleet. After the revolution of 1917 and the withdrawal of Russia from the war after the treaty of Brest Litovsk, the situation in the country became extremely confused. Strong "White" (anti-Bolshevik) forces existed in northern Russia, eventually coming together under the leadership of Admiral Kolchak. These included the Czech Legion which had become stranded in Russia. In the south, General Denikin seemed to have the potential to overthrow the Leninist "Red" regime. The White forces were riven by internal squabbles however, and the loyalty of their troops was always questionable in the face of the formidable propaganda machine of the Communists. At the same time the German armies were withdrawing from Russian and Baltic territories after their rapid advances in 1917, leaving behind them a chaotic situation. In Poland and the Baltic States fierce fighting continued even after the Treaty of Versailles had made its best efforts to settle international boundaries.

Into the murky waters of the Russian civil war, Britain and her Allies unwisely plunged. Troops had been stationed around the White Sea to defend stores dumped there, originally destined for the Tsarist Russian Army. These troops had to be either evacuated in 1919 or resupplied and supported. At the same time, under the influence of Churchill, now Minister of Defence, somewhat half-hearted efforts were made to assist the anti-Bolshevik forces. The British establishment naturally hated the Communist led government which had emerged in Moscow and pulled Russia out of the war, murdering the Tsar and his family. Communism itself was a doctrine repulsive to the ruling classes in Britain and if it could be overcome by stiffening the White forces with some experienced British soldiers and marines backed by warships, so much the better. This was a misguided and irresponsible policy and involved becoming mixed up with some extremely unsavoury characters (Kolchak was a particularly bloodthirsty individual). The monitors were to play a significant role in its execution.

The port of Murmansk on the Kola Peninsula was a crucial entry point to northern Russia, and was connected to the rest of the country by a railway leading down the western side of the White Sea through the small port of Kem (see map 6). The White Sea itself was open to shipping only in the summer months but had great strategic importance as it gave access to the shallow but navigable river systems of the Dvina and the Onega, which in turn connected to the railway network at Kotias and Vologta respectively. Archangel, at the mouth of the Dvina, was a most important city and arsenal. As the roads in northern Russia were impassable most of the year, these communication links were vital to any military operation.

British minesweepers and other small ships had been active in the area since 1915 protecting merchant shipping and preventing the Germans from using the northern route to threaten the right flank of Russian forces in Europe. In July

1918 these small ships were joined by *M23* and *M25* to strengthen the position of troops protecting British military stores and to keep the northern ports closed to German forces, which might otherwise be evacuated northward through Finland and sent to the western front. At that point most of northern Russia was in "White" hands and the Czech Legion was actively supporting the "Whites" from its Siberian base. *M23* initially was sent to Kem, where she joined up with a small Allied contingent sent there to protect the railway running south from Murmansk, which was threatened by Red forces. *M25* went directly to Archangel and then moved cautiously up the shallow waters of the Dvina to back up a joint British and Commonwealth force which had advanced southwards up the river, driving a Red force, supported by some improvised river gunboats, before it. The gunboats had seriously hampered the British advance, but the arrival of the monitor with her 7.5 inch gun changed the situation dramatically. She was able to use her main armament and her secondary batteries to chase off the gunboats and destroy the Red Army's light artillery, so as to enable the troops to renew their advance, and, most importantly, prepare their positions for the fearsome Russian winter which was to come. During some spirited actions she sunk a Russian gunboat but was hit herself by a shell which damaged her slightly, caused four fatalities and left seven men wounded.

It was now autumn and the river would soon be impassable due to ice so the monitor had to withdraw to Archangel for the winter. Here she could be relatively comfortable, and her crew, as they celebrated the Armistice in November, no doubt felt sorry for the soldiers who had slogged through the mud in the mosquito ridden northern summer and were now enduring the bitter cold winter, harassed by Bolshevik forces, and constantly threatened by Russian traitors in their midst.

Two more 7.5 inch monitors, *M24* and *M26* together with some China gunboats joined the small force, the gunboats having the advantage of much shallower draft. At first it was decided to use the ships to cover the evacuation of the British force, the war in western Europe having now ceased, but some successes further south by Kolchak's forces prompted Churchill to continue the campaign, and *Humber, M27, M33* and *M31* set off in the spring of 1919 to give support. *M23* was the first to see action, responding to a threat that the "Reds" might overrun the beleaguered force on the Dvina, she blasted her way through the ice of the river in early May and brought welcome support to the troops on the ground before the "Reds" could deploy their forces. She was followed closely by the China gunboats.

A major offensive now took place in which the monitors tried to force their way further up river to the railhead at Kotlas where they hoped to link up with White forces further south. The river was shallow, beset by sandbanks and very bendy, the bends making spotting for gunfire difficult, however kite balloons and even a few aircraft were available and much expertise in making use of indirect fire from the monitors had been acquired off the Belgian coast. The force was thus able to advance slowly up river. It became apparent that the most effective ships in this situation were the *Humber* with her battery of three 6 inch guns and lightly armoured hull, and *M27* now fitted with triple 4 inch guns and able to achieve a very high rate of fire. These ships had the advantage of drawing less water than the larger gunned monitors and being much more robust than the gunboats. The advance progressed well until the Russian troops accompanying the

British force decided to change their allegiance and, with typical Bolshevik delicacy, murdered their own officers and any British ones they could lay their hands on. This reversal of fortune gave the "Reds" an opportunity to launch a strong counter attack. The monitors had a hard fight to stabilise the situation and drive their erstwhile allies away from positions from which they could pose a threat. It was now obvious however that the British troops would have to withdraw, but as the river level was too low for the ships to get back to Archangel, they had to continue the fight until conditions improved. As they did so more and more Russians defected to the "Reds", fearful of falling victim to the atrocities which so distinguished the Red Army when it came to grips with opposing forces. Further south Kolchak's forces were also beginning to crumble. Eventually the river level rose a little and the long suffering troops and their equipment were loaded into barges and sent downriver. The monitors had to dump some of their armament and their protective armour to reduce their draft and then conducted a safe withdrawal except for *M27* and *M25*. These were totally disarmed and then blown up as they could not clear the shallows.

While these dramatic events were in progress on the Dvina, *M24*, *M26*, joined by *M23*, which had come back down- river after her initial charge through the ice, were busy in the White Sea. Russians around the White Sea ports of Onega, Kandalaksha and Kem mutinied and handed the towns over to the "Reds", leaving small British contingents in both places at great risk. These had to be evacuated and then heavy gun support provided to White troops trying to recapture Onega. *Erebus* had by this time been sent up from Portsmouth to join the squadron and used her main armament to attempt to dislodge the "Reds", but in spite of over

100 15-inch rounds, the enemy held on. This final action had been a failure and there was now no alternative but to withdraw all British forces from northern Russia and bring the monitors home. The ships were able to reassemble safely in Archangel and commence the voyage back to Britain, the small monitors making the passage under tow.

Erebus's work was not over however. As she was steaming home she was ordered to the Baltic where the Estonians and Latvians were joined with the "Whites" fighting against Bolshevik forces around in the Gulf of Finland. She started by ineffectively bombarding forts protecting St Petersburg, then, short of ammunition, retired to meet up with a supply ship where she was able to re-arm. By this time the "Whites" attacking St Petersburg had almost given up and there seemed to be no point in offering them further support. The British Baltic Flotilla, to which she was attached, now turned its attention to Latvia, to which there was a threat from both the successful Red Russian forces and from the German "Iron Division" which, in defiance of the Treaty of Versailles, was launching an attack on Poland and the Baltic states. It seemed that Latvia was in danger of collapsing in the face of two such powerful enemies and Britain became involved to enforce the League of Nations guarantees of Latvian independence. On 9 November *Erebus* opened fire on German forces advancing on Libau (Leipaja) on the Latvian coast, driving them back with the support of the fire of cruisers and destroyers. Shortly afterwards the Germans attacked again in strength but were met by a ferocious counter attack mounted by the Latvians and covered by a "creeping barrage" from the guns of *Erebus* and the smaller vessels. They were firing at very close range over open sights and the effect of *Erebus*'s shells, weighing almost a ton each, must have been devastating to the German troops. They were routed and did not attack again. *Erebus* remained on guard off the coast until the ice forced her to leave the Baltic in December. Her mission had been successful. The Germans did not attempt to attack again until the Second World War and the independence of this small state had been, at least for a time, assured. The Latvians were loud in their praises for what they called "the mighty British nation and her wise government".

Unlike this brief episode in the Baltic, the White Sea campaign had been unpopular at home and had been particularly hard for the troops on the ground, who knew that their colleagues in France were now home and demobilised, but the monitors had certainly saved them from an unpleasant fate at the hands of the "Reds". Learning from the lessons in the art of indirect fire learnt off the Belgian coast they had deployed their guns with devastating accuracy and efficiency, inflicting heavy casualties and severe material damage on the enemy. They had also been handled with great courage and skill, under the leadership of Captain E. Altham RN, who commanded the naval forces. Altham had previously been captain of *Crauford* and in this role had done much of the work on developing communication between spotting aircraft and monitors. He was a resourceful and popular officer.

In southern Russia, General Denikin's forces were deployed in fertile plains on the shores of the Black Sea and in the Crimea. The "Reds", however soon gained the upper-hand and confined them to the Kerch Peninsula in the eastern Crimea and the mainland around Krasnodar, (see map 7). Some British naval forces had been in the Black Sea since late 1918, and in March 1919, *M17* and *M18*, both still fitted with their formidable if slow firing 9.2 inch main armament, were sent to the Crimea. The campaign promised to offer exactly the sort of work they were intended for, supporting ground troops close to the shore, working in shallow water. Neither the "Reds" nor the "Whites" had much in the way of a navy so interference by hostile ships was not expected. Their first operation was an attack on shore batteries close to Sevastopol, which was successfully carried out, then the ships moved round into the Sea of Azov to support White forces fighting to retain a hold on the Kerch Peninsula. The monitors engaged the left flank of Red forces advancing from the west, while cruisers in the Black Sea bombarded the right. Their effect was soon felt as shells fell on the advancing troops and crucially on the railway facilities on which the Red Army depended for supplies. Soon they were joined by M29, armed with two 6 inch guns and capable of a much higher rate of fire. M17 suffered some damage, not from the enemy but from the recoil of her own guns and had to return to Mudros, M22 steamed out to replace her. The fire from the ships put new heart into the White forces and soon most of the Crimea was under their control, so the monitors were moved northwards to Genichesk close to the neck of the Crimean Peninsula. Here they harassed Red forces and communications while Denikin consolidated his grip on land. Briefly it looked as if, at least in southern Russia, the "Whites" might triumph. Denikin's army spread out into the Ukraine and the Kuban driving the "Reds" before it. In order to support the White armies in Ukraine it was important to control the mouths of the rivers Bug and Dnestr, and the railheads at Nikolajev and Odessa so that and armed barges loaded with supplies could move up river in support of the advancing White armies. M22 and M29 were moved to the north western sector of the Black Sea to provide support and in August they opened fire on the forts at Nikolajev, at the mouth of the Bug, which soon fell into White hands. Odessa then surrendered without waiting to be bombarded, opening the way to the mouth of the Dnestr, and the railway into the interior. Denikin however was no match for Trotsky as a strategist. He attempted a march on Moscow, running too far ahead of his supply train. His army was defeated and routed at Oryol in October. By that time the monitors had been withdrawn from the Black Sea, and they took no further part in the Russian Civil War which continued into 1920 when the last of the White forces managed to withdraw from the Crimea.

It is interesting that in these interventions in Russia, the Royal Navy used only the small monitors (apart from the brief involvement of *Erebus*), which proved impressively formidable against land based forces. The little ships were cheap to operate, reasonably reliable and small enough to be considered expendable. They could also creep up shallow rivers, just as the American river monitors had in the 1860s, providing vital heavy gun support to troops operating inland. The great guns in the large monitors were really only necessary when the ships were opposed by long range heavy coastal batteries, as was the case in Belgium. The 4 inch, 6 inch and 9.2 inch guns were quite big enough to overwhelm enemy field artillery and had the range to reach almost 10 miles inland, enabling them to dominate coastal and riverine towns and railheads. Multiple 6 inch and 4 inch batteries on the small monitors were particularly devastating to troops on shore as they could achieve such a high rate of fire, *M27's* 4 inch battery for example could deliver fifty rounds per minute, enough to destroy any army formation not safely dug in with good top cover.

The end of the Great War brought a sharp reduction in naval strength, to which the monitor fleet was by no means immune. Of the three remaining 14 inch gunned ships (*Raglan* having been sunk), two were scrapped soon after the war. One, *Roberts*, was used for various experimental purposes until 1936 when she followed her sisters to the scrap yard. All but one of the 12 inch ships went the same way, the survivor being *Clive*. She had her 18 inch turret removed and replaced by an even more monstrous weapon, a triple 15 inch mounting which was intended as a prototype for the armament of a new class of battle cruiser. When the trials were completed the turret was removed and she was scrapped. The new triple 15 inch battle cruisers were never built. The fate of the 15 inch monitors was more interesting. There was at first a plan to move all of them except the unmanageable *Ney* to Singapore to protect the vast naval base under construction there. This idea was eventually abandoned and land based heavy artillery provided instead. It is interesting to speculate how this decision affected the disaster which befell the colony in 1942. If the monitors had managed to survive Japanese bombers they might have made it much more difficult for the Japanese to advance down the Malay Peninsula and cross the causeway to Singapore. As it was various fortunes awaited the ships. *Ney*, the most unfortunate of all of them, was for a time a depot ship for small craft and an accommodation hulk at Portsmouth but ended her days at Devonport where she provided accommodation and facilities for a training establishment until 1957. *Soult* which, with her Vickers diesel engine, had been a very successful and hard worked warship and was put to good use, at first as a gunnery training ship, used mainly to teach seamen turret drills. Her 15 inch turret was an excellent and reliable unit, in stark contrast to some of the later British turret designs. It was almost identical to those used on the *Queen Elizabeth* class battleships and on the various battle cruisers which survived to serve in the Second World War, so *Soult*'s guns provided a very useful training ground. When the Second World War became imminent and Churchill returned to the Admiralty as First Lord, he was keen to recommission the monitors which had, he thought, been his own brain children. Plans to re-engine and refit *Soult* were drawn up, but it soon became clear that a completely new ship was a more sensible option. Accordingly she was put to use as an accommodation ship and later, in 1940, her turret was removed so as to be fitted onto a new monitor. *Soult* herself was then used as a depot ship for small vessels at Chatham, providing repair, administrative and maintenance facilities. During the Blitz in early 1941 it became apparent that her armoured decks made her impervious to German general purpose bombs, one of which hit her squarely on the foredeck but did only minimal damage. This made her popular as a floating air raid shelter. She was finally broken up in 1946.

Erebus and *Terror* were of course relatively new ships and in an entirely different class as far as performance was concerned. After *Erebus*'s Baltic adventure both ships were attached to the Chatham gunnery school and both were intermittently employed on various tests of guns and ammunition, firing at targets which included the surrendered German battleship *Baden*. *Terror* was then re-fitted and sent on a mission to Singapore where she acted as guard ship from 1933 until the outbreak of the war. *Erebus* was offered to South Africa to counter local fears of a Japanese invasion; she was to be crewed partly by South Africans and partly by

Royal Navy personnel wearing rather comical South African uniforms. She was just ready to leave when the war broke out and the mission was cancelled. In both these roles the monitors were supposed to operate in an anti-ship role for which they had never been intended, and, with their slow speed, were inherently unsuitable. Luckily they were never called upon to prove the truth that shore bombardment is an entirely different affair to sea fighting. Three 15 inch monitors might have deterred Japanese troops moving down the coast road towards Singapore, but a single one would have stood no chance at all in a sea fight against the superb gunnery and fighting skills of the Imperial Japanese Navy.

Gorgon, the sole surviving ex-Norwegian coastal defence ship with her unusual armament was no use to the Royal Navy, or to the Norwegians. She was offered for sale in various quarters, the most promising of which was Romania, but everything fell through and she was quickly scrapped.

Severn, Humber and *Mersey* had done excellent service but after the White Sea campaign (which only *Humber* actually reached before the evacuation) the navy had no use for them and they were sold for scrap. *Humber* did have another life however as she was converted into a crane barge in Holland and used to dismantle obsolete ships and wrecks for various owners until 1939.

The small M class monitors, being extremely simple and built to merchant ship standards were altogether a different proposition. Eight of them were bought by the Shell company and converted into small tankers, mainly being employed in Venezuela to ship crude oil around Lake Maracaibo, later the hulls were used for bunkering duties in various places. The rest of the ships were retained for a time by the Royal Navy for various training duties and as coastal minelayers. In these roles they were graced with names and remained in service until the late 1930s. Three survived long enough to see service in the Second World War, one, *Melpomene,* was fitted with a torpedo tube and used as a torpedo instruction vessel and another, *Medusa,* received a heavy winch and was used as a tender and depot ship for submarines and small craft. *Minerva* (ex *M33)* became a small accommodation vessel and was eventually restored to her original configuration and can still be seen in Portsmouth.

Chapter 7

The Second World War – The Mediterranean Phase One

*P*acem vis bellum parare (If you wish for peace prepare for war) is one of the wisest of classical mottos. Britain, during the "long weekend" between the two world wars, preferred to search for peace by throwing away its weapons, starving its armed forces of resources and imagining in a cloud of myopic optimism that other nations would do the same. Nowhere was this more true than in naval policy. While the fascist powers built fast, powerful new battleships, Britain depended on slow outdated vessels laid down during, or even before, the First World War. Her two *Nelson* class battleships, the only ones completed in the inter war period, virtually had their stern sections cut off to comply with treaty restrictions, and were so underpowered that they could barely keep up with their pre-1918 sisters. Worst of all, reorganisation of the armed forces left Britain, which had had by far the most advanced naval aviation in the world in 1918, with no modern naval aircraft at all and with the Fleet Air Arm and Coastal Command reduced to little more than token forces. The monitor force, obsolete though it was, had to bear some of the consequences of these failures of national will and prudence. As the ships often operated singly it is easiest to follow the careers of each of the four 15 inch ships which participated in the Second World War separately.

The outbreak of war found *Terror* refitting in Singapore. The barrels of her main armament were replaced by a part worn pair from the old battleship *Revenge* and she was equipped with six 4 inch high angle AA guns. At this stage she had no radar and was consequently very vulnerable to air attack. As there was no fighting at the time in the Far East, the Admiralty decided to bring her home to the Channel, perhaps to repeat the coastal bombardments which had been such a feature of the monitor's activity in the past. The "phoney war" however meant that there was nothing much happening in western Europe so as she made her leisurely way home she was diverted to another sphere of conflict. Most Royal Navy warships, including three battleships and an aircraft carrier, had been withdrawn from the Mediterranean to home waters at the outbreak of war, leaving Malta and Alexandria very poorly protected. Only four small cruisers, a handful of Australian destroyers and a few gunboats remained in the Med. Italy was not yet involved in the war, but it seemed very likely that she soon would be, and she had a modern and extremely powerful fleet. Mussolini had made no secret of his ambition to get control of the British colony of Malta, with its great harbour and dockyards. *Terror* was thus sent in March 1940 to supplement the island's defences, which at that time consisted of only a few obsolete 9.2 inch guns and a handful of AA weapons. She was moored in Lazaretto Creek, just behind

Manoel Island, close to the Grand Harbour. The ancient, odd looking ship at first became quite a joke on the island, lurking in her creek, great guns facing seawards. Italy declared war on Britain on 10 June 1940, as soon as Mussolini became convinced that France was on the point of defeat. He was hoping to participate in a division of the spoils but instead suffered a naval bombardment of his naval bases by British and French ships. It was however only about 50 miles from Malta to Sicily where modern Italian bombers were based and a day after war broke out some 250 enemy aircraft appeared over Malta. These were high level bombers, very difficult to hit with anti-aircraft fire, but at the same time very inaccurate in their own aim. *Terror* was in action against them almost every day from June until September, when the arrival of more land based guns on the island allowed her a respite. In November she moved to Suda Bay in Crete which was being used as an advanced base for British forces trying to help the Greeks to repel the Italian invasion of their country. Once again her activity was entirely in an anti-aircraft role and continued until land based AA guns were installed.

Pre-war British strategy as regards the Mediterranean had been based on the assumption that the French navy would play a major role in the western part of that sea, as it had in the First World War. Together with a relatively small British contingent in the east, the French would be able to keep the Italian fleet at bay and maintain the vital communication link to the Suez Canal, the oil reserves of the Persian Gulf and the Empire east of Suez. The collapse of France and consequent disengagement of almost all her navy made it extremely difficult for Britain to maintain any effective presence in the region, indeed if the Italians, with their magnificent new battle fleet, had shown a reasonable amount of aggression, the Royal Navy would have had to abandon the Middle Sea altogether. Churchill nevertheless continually pressed for an aggressive stance, including schemes for the capture of the Italian island of Pantellaria, which the chiefs of staff were able to quash, and the invasion of Dakar, mainly by Gaullist French forces transported and supported by the Royal Navy. This operation did go ahead and was a complete failure, resulting in severe losses to an already overstretched navy.

Notwithstanding all these problems, the War Cabinet, at Churchill's insistence, refused to abandon the Mediterranean, against the advice of the First Lord of the Admiralty, Sir Dudley Pound. During the summer of 1940 the British fleet at Alexandria was gradually built up under the aggressive and capable leadership of Admiral Sir Andrew Cunningham. Its first major action in July 1940 set the pattern for the first part of the campaign. A powerful Italian force of battleships and heavy cruisers was intercepted and put to flight just south of Sicily by Cunningham's obsolescent battleships and light cruisers. Although no major Italian ships were sunk, their morale suffered a blow from which it never recovered. But the action taught Cunningham a salutary lesson. Italian bombers had plagued the British relentlessly and although only one ship, the cruiser *Gloucester*, was damaged, the others escaped only by luck. They had inadequate deck armour and poor AA defences. His only carrier *Eagle*, also unarmoured, had a complement of seventeen Swordfish torpedo bombers and only two obsolete Gladiator bi-plane fighters. In an astonishing exercise of wishful thinking the navy had convinced itself that warships needed almost no fighter protection. Gallant though the efforts of Fleet Air Arm fighter pilots were, they could provide no effective defence against massed enemy air attack unless properly equipped with sufficient numbers of modern fighters. Until this was done, sending valuable warships within range of enemy aircraft was to invite disaster.

But some warships were not so valuable. The North African coast from Alexandria to Tripoli (see map 8) is low and sparsely populated for almost 1,000 miles, and close to the coast runs a single road along which are situated the only significant towns and settlements. The desert inland consists of soft rolling sand dunes and patches of harder soil baked dry by the sun. It is almost impassable for wheeled vehicles and difficult going even for tanks. Any large movement of troops or supplies has to move along the coast road, and is therefore vulnerable to naval bombardment. These are exactly the conditions which monitors were designed to exploit. It would, as Cunningham had learnt, have been foolhardy to risk a valuable battleship close to a hostile coast, exposed to enemy air attack, submarines and mines, but an ancient monitor and a few river gunboats was a different matter. Cunningham had always been insistent that the navy should be unstinting in its support of the army. He actually described the army as "A projectile fired by the navy". He was about to be able to show how seriously he took the role.

In December 1940 General, Sir Richard O'Connor had launched a counter attack on Italian forces which had pushed into Egypt, and within days the Italians were put to flight, the British force of 31,000 men making no less than 130,000 Italians captive. *Terror* and the gunboats *Aphis* and *Ladybird* were involved from the start in this remarkable performance. Swordfish aircraft from Alexandria acted as spotters. The bombardment opened with an attack by the ships on Maktila from about 10 miles offshore, then the retreating Italians were harried as they fled westward through the small port of Sollum. The Italians replied, using their field artillery against the small bombardment squadron, but the range was too great for them and *Terror* was able to silence batteries whilst the smaller ships close inshore harried the retreating army. After two days, and the expenditure of over 200 rounds, *Terror* had to return to Alexandria for more ammunition then turned her attention to Bardia, the easternmost town in Libya, right on the enemy line of retreat. For three days, as the unfortunate Italians were fleeing through the town, they were subjected to the fire of the gunboats and the monitor, now joined by two Australian destroyers. Once again *Terror* shot up the heavy enemy defensive artillery from long range allowing the smaller ships to shell the town itself and the harbour. Enemy aircraft tried to intervene but the ships were not hit. One of the worries during this engagement was the condition of *Terror*'s gun barrels which had been part worn when she had them fitted in Singapore. Cunningham himself came aboard to inspect them. To minimise wear, three quarter charges of cordite were used for this relatively close range work. As soon as Sollum fell into British hands *Terror* assumed the role of anti-aircraft picket, occasionally breaking off to ferry stores from Alexandria.

Early in January it was Bardia's turn to fall to O'Connor's army which was again supported by heavy fire from the Inshore Squadron, as the monitor, gunboats and destroyers were now called, and now also from Cunningham's battleships which risked the short run from Alexandria to join the bombardment. The newly arrived carrier *Illustrious* provided air cover but once again there was a shortage of fighters and the Italian air attacks were heavy. *Terror* was in the thick of the fighting and shot down at least one bomber. The town fell on 5 January.

There was now nothing of significance between the British and Tobruk, which had a useful seaport. Once again the Inshore Squadron was called upon to soften up the objective. By now *Terror*'s guns were in a sorry state, having fired over 600 rounds per barrel – far beyond their prescribed limit. The effect was that the shells, instead of being stabilised by the gyroscopic effect of the rotation imparted by the rifling in the barrel, wobbled and somersaulted in the air and often cartwheeled along the ground before exploding. They were still extremely frightening to anyone on the receiving end, but accurate fire was impossible. In the absence of replacement barrels she had to be relegated to guardship duties outside Tobruk , once again facing heavy air attack. Her AA armament was beefed up with some captured Italian 20mm guns but she was still without radar, depending on the eyes and ears of watchkeepers to warn of imminent attack. On 16 February she escorted a convoy westwards to Benghazi, which had fallen a few days earlier. Lying outside the port she was subjected to savage air attacks, not just from the Italians but from German bombers which had recently arrived in Sicily. These were an entirely different kettle of fish. Italian airmen certainly didn't lack courage but their technique for bombing and torpedo attack was poor and their leadership deficient. By contrast the Luftwaffe were expert in anti-ship warfare. In particular Fliegerkorps X, the formation established in Sicily, were the greatest exponents of the art of warship busting. Their JU87 (Stuka) dive bombers were very vulnerable to fighters and could not operate against strong defences, but they were a devastating weapon when used against an exposed target like a lone ship. Diving almost vertically on their prey, Stukas were very difficult to shoot down and could deliver their bombs with great accuracy. Three near misses by German bombs damaged *Terror* on 22 February, splitting open her bulges and causing leaks into the magazines. She could still steam and was ordered to return to Alexandria escorted by a corvette and a minesweeper. As she steamed close inshore she set off two magnetic mines which caused further hull damage and flooding. The next day she was provided with air cover by a lone Hurricane fighter, but at about 1800hrs it departed to refuel and soon five Stukas appeared with their own fighter escort. The Stukas came in from the starboard quarter, where only two 4 inch and two 20mm guns would bear and their bombs exploded close alongside *Terror* causing the hull to buckle and split aft of the turret. Oil fuel caught fire and water flooded into the hull extinguishing the furnaces and putting the pumps and generators out of action. An attempt to tow was found to be useless so all the crew except the anti-aircraft gunners and the senior officers were evacuated. The ship continued to settle in the water and eventually the seacocks were opened and depth charges exploded to send her to the bottom, about 20 miles north west of Derna. All of her complement were safely taken aboard the escorts. Her captain, Commander H. J. Haynes was the last to leave the ship.

So ended the life of a gallant old ship which, unmodernised, had been plunged into a war for which she was obviously ill equipped. She had nevertheless played her part with spirit and skill, doing exactly what she had been intended to do when she was launched 25 years earlier. Her support for the troops on the ground had been invaluable and her status as a disposable asset had enabled her to undertake risks which would have been unacceptable for any other big gun ship.

Erebus had been on the point of setting out for South Africa when the war broke out. The South African members of her crew were not at all sure where their loyalties lay, many of them favouring Germany over their former colonial masters. With difficulty the South African Government were persuaded to release Britain from her undertaking to loan the ship to them, so her South African crew were sent home. Churchill was keen that she should be used immediately to repeat the performance of the monitors in 1914, but this was not to be. She was in no condition to operate close to enemy coasts and the Admiralty had the good sense to keep her in a training role until extensive modifications could be made. Early in 1940 she was taken in hand by Thornycroft's yard in Southampton and considerably modified. Her deck armour was increased from 2 inches to 4 over vulnerable spots to make her less prone to bomb attack, and extensive new AA armament was provided. Six 4 inch high angle guns were fitted together with four quadruple 0.5 inch machine guns. She was also provided with a strange new weapon, in the form of two twenty-barrel rocket launchers. These fired rockets which ejected parachute flares to which were attached small explosive mines at the end of long cables. The idea was that these would be deployed as aircraft attacked, and the cable would become entangled with the aircraft, drawing the mine onto it. This seemed a good idea but the device in practice proved more dangerous to the ship than to its attackers. For example, it is likely that *Hood* was damaged by the explosion of her own anti-aircraft rockets during her fatal encounter with *Bismarck*. At the same time degaussing cables to protect from magnetic mines were fitted, the bulwarks were raised and the mast height reduced. Thus modified she steamed up to the Orkneys to conduct crew training before going into action.

By the time *Erebus* was ready for action the Germans had overrun Belgium and Holland and powerful air forces made it unwise to risk even a monitor close to the enemy coast, but Churchill was keen to do as much damage to the German held channel ports as possible and to harass enemy gun emplacements being set up on the French coast. In September 1940, at the height of the Battle of Britain, the old monitor set off unescorted to do battle with the all-conquering Wehrmacht. Off Lowestoft she encountered a patrol of enemy E-boats, fast motor torpedo craft, who fired two torpedoes at her. They all missed ahead, probably the Germans could not believe that a warship making so much wash could only be travelling at 9 knots. (The wash was greatly increased by the ship's side bulges, now under water due to the increased weight of the armour plate and secondary armament recently fitted). A solitary enemy bomber attacked later, in the Thames Estuary, making the same mistake. *Erebus*'s first operational mission, however, was a failure, she was ordered to bombard barges being prepared for Operation *Sealion*, the German invasion of Britain, but she was unable to reach her prescribed firing position, being so difficult to steer that she could not keep in the narrow swept channel through the coastal minefields. The next day, with the help of a tug, she made it to the buoy which was laid to mark her firing position, sighted 8 miles east of the South Goodwin lightship, dropped anchor and began to bombard Calais docks, but after a few rounds trouble with the gun turrets, and the absence of reports from the Swordfish aircraft which were supposed to be spotting the fall of shot, forced her to stop. Further operations were delayed until the middle of October due to poor weather and freshly laid mine-fields, but on the 16th she opened accurate fire at a range of 25,000 yards (a little over 14 statute miles) on Dunkirk docks. Oddly enough she was accompanied on this occasion by the same tug, *Lady Brassey*, which she had worked with 25 years earlier. There were no large enemy ships in Dunkirk at the time so no serious damage was done.

Admiral Ramsay, the commander-in-chief Dover, was not at all satisfied with *Erebush*'s performance and had her sent to Chatham then to Tilbury for modifications, including the fitting of a larger rudder, in the hope that this would make her more controllable, and a type 91 radar jammer. She was then stationed at Southend to ward off enemy mine laying aircraft. Her next aggressive mission was to bombard the submarine pens at Ostend assisted again by a Swordfish spotter. Several good hits were made on the pens but no damage to submarines was reported. Life must have been uncomfortable in the harbour area however as the 15 inch shells rained down. At that point in the war RAF bombing was neither accurate nor effective so it was good to show a little aggressive action from the sea.

Erebus however was still not a satisfactory ship. She still had no radar and her general efficiency was considered to be poor with too many breakdowns. Her crew also was not up to full strength which made it difficult to put matters right. It was clear to all concerned that in the age of aircraft and coastal radar, the idea of using her consistently to bombard the Belgian coast as she had in 1918, was not viable. She was dismissed from the Dover Command and sent up to Scotland to re-train and take on a full complement.

Affairs in North Africa had taken a dramatic turn for the worse since the loss of *Terror*. German forces, supported by a powerful air force contingent, had checked the British advance and, under the leadership of General Erwin Rommel, then advanced remorselessly eastwards, driving towards Egypt and the Suez Canal. In April Tobruk was besieged and the British, weakened by the diversion of some 50,000 men and many aircraft in a futile attempt to save Greece from the advancing Germans, were everywhere pushed back. The Royal Navy suffered one of its worst wartime disasters when German bombers destroyed much of the Mediterranean fleet as it attempted to evacuate British forces from Crete. The appearance of U-boats in the Mediterranean in addition to the formidable Axis air forces, threatened to make it impossible for the British to maintain the vital strategic island of Malta. Admiral Cunningham managed to keep the garrison at Tobruk supplied by sea until December, losing twenty-seven ships in the process, and at the end of the year the garrison had to be withdrawn. It had not passed without notice that the presence of a monitor in the Mediterranean might have been a useful addition to the hard pressed naval forces there and help the army to check the advance of Rommel's forces. The Admiralty now had two such ships available, *Erebus* and the newly completed *Roberts*. The two met up in Loch Foyle and with an escort of a sloop and a corvette, set off on 1 December 1941 to join the Mediterranean Fleet by way of the Cape of Good Hope. Awaiting *Erebus* in South Africa, however there were new orders.

The battleship *Prince of Wales* and the battle cruiser *Repulse* had been sunk by Japanese aircraft on 10 December after a combination of carelessness and stupidity had left them without air cover within range of the most expert naval air arm in the world. Fearing that Japan's next objective might be India, the Admiralty diverted *Erebus* to Trincomalee in Ceylon (now known as Sri Lanka). After their successes in the first months of the war the Japanese seemed poised for an attack on the island which was the base of the British fleet in the Indian Ocean. Luckily the British was able to read most of Japan's naval signals and had some warning that an attack was imminent in early April. To avoid the same fate as that which befell *Prince of Wales* and *Repulse,* Admiral, Sir James Somerville withdrew the main elements of his force, including two fast aircraft carriers *Indomitable* and *Formidable,* to the Maldives. On 5 April the first Japanese strike came with 125 bombers and torpedo aircraft making a landfall at Galle and flying up the west coast of the island towards Colombo. In spite of the presence of radar and the fact that thousands of people saw the raiders arrive over the island, the RAF and Australian fighter squadrons at Colombo were caught off guard. Two cruisers at sea and one old ship in harbour were sunk together with a destroyer, and twenty-seven aircraft were destroyed, mostly on the ground. Japanese losses are uncertain, probably about ten aircraft destroyed by flack.

On 9 April it was Trincomalee's turn. *Hermes,* an old, slow, aircraft carrier, had put to sea to avoid the anticipated attack, but the Japanese found her and sunk her and her two escorts. Fortunately no aircraft were on board. The attack on the town itself was less successful due to heavy flack and some fighter protection. Eleven Japanese aircraft were shot down for the loss of eight Australian Hurricanes and one Fleet Air Arm Fulmar. *Erebus* played a spirited part in the air defence. She suffered minor damage by near misses from six bombs along her port side. Five men were killed and twenty wounded by splinters. It was the last serious attack on Ceylon of the war.

Although the British expected further attacks and moved their fleet to safer waters off east Africa, the Japanese decided that they had more important fields to conquer (as they thought). The carriers *Akagi, Ryujo, Hiyu* and *Soryu*, which had spearheaded the attack on the island, withdrew eastwards to their own rendezvous with destiny at the great Battle of Midway Island in June, leaving Ceylon in relative peace.

Exactly what Their Lordships had expected the First World War monitor do to deter the Japanese from attacking Ceylon is difficult to determine, but after the withdrawal of the British fleet to east Africa there was clearly no role for her there and she was sent to Mombasa to join the rest of the fleet. There had been some suggestion that she should then take up duties as guardship at the mouth of the Persian Gulf, but this idea was abandoned when it was decided to attack Madagascar, then held by the Vichy French. Landings were made at Diego Suarez in the north of the island and at Majunga, further west. *Erebus* was part of the force sent to bombard Majunga in support of the landing by troops and Royal Marines but she got no chance to use her main armament. Resistance was light and heavy gun support was not required. After a short period as guardship off Madagascar the old warrior was sent to Durban where she briefly reverted to her role as turret drill ship, and had her ancient boilers re-tubed. It was not until April 1943 that she resumed her much interrupted journey to the Mediterranean.

By this time British forces had chased Rommel out of Libya and Axis forces in North Africa were on the point of surrender. They had been defeated largely because British air and seaborne forces had been able to sever Rommel's supply lines from Europe, starving him of men, supplies and most importantly, petrol. It is amusing to think that while fighting in Libya, Rommel's tanks were driving unknowingly over one of the richest oil fields in the world. Victorious now in Africa, the Allies were planning to invade Sicily and the support of every heavy gun available, including those of *Erebus*, would be needed to ensure success of the most dangerous and difficult of military operations – landing forces from the sea in the face of well prepared defences.

The voyage to the Med through the Suez Cannel was not without incident. *Erebus*'s reluctance to go straight made her impossible to handle in the narrow waters of the canal and she twice blundered into the banks, damaging her rudder. She was pulled off and set off again with a tug at bow and stern, then had to be dry docked for repairs to her rudder and bottom. She was however ready to join her younger sisters *Roberts* and *Abercrombie* (we shall hear more of their activities in a later chapter) in time for the great invasion of southern Europe. At last the old girl was to be employed in the very task which she had been designed to perform.

Operation *Huskey*, (see map 9) as the Allied invasion of Sicily was called, got off to a bad start. Planning on the naval side was the responsibility of the admirable Admiral Ramsay who was a superb planner of combined operations involving all three services, and, in this case, the US Army and Navy as well, but at every turn he was frustrated by the pig headed-ness and personal vanity of senior officers (British and American) wanting to score points for themselves. Eventually, however, plans for landing 115,000 British and 66,000 American troops, all in the south east of the island, were finalised, and thanks to Ramsay's meticulous planning all went reasonably well. The first action was to capture the tiny islands of Pantellaria and Lampedusa which were heavily bombed from the air then bombarded by cruisers so as to soften them up before troops were landed. There was said to be only one Allied serious casualty in this operation – a British soldier badly bitten by a donkey.

Over 2,500 ships, some from North Africa, some from Britain and some direct from the USA, converged on the Sicilian landing beaches in good order, in spite of challenging weather conditions. Patton's army advanced rapidly on Palermo and then along the north coast, driving the outnumbered but undefeated defenders before it. *Abercrombie's* part in this operation is described later. Montgomery had a much tougher struggle in the east of the island, pushing slowly forward towards Catania, but the Italians now began the process of dismissing Mussolini and withdrawing from the war, so Hitler determined to withdraw his army in good order from Sicily and fight a delaying campaign, tying up as many Allied forces as possible, as he retreated slowly up the Italian peninsular under the skilful generalship of "Smiling Albert" Kesselring. This, he hoped would prevent, or at least delay, Allied intervention in Western Europe.

This Italian campaign promised to provide excellent opportunities for monitors to work with forces on land. The Italian fleet was unlikely to intervene and although there was always a danger of attack by some of the 4-500 German aircraft based in or near Sicily, these were heavily outnumbered by Allied sea and land based machines. One of the benefits of having good air cover was that it allowed better observation of long range bombardments. Instead of Swordfish, the monitors had now learnt to work with Spitfires in the spotting role. The Spitfire, with its excellent visibility, made quite a good spotter, although the job was not popular with pilots, the major problem being communi-

cation. RAF radios used different frequencies and procedures to ships and although lengthy rehearsals were carried
out both aircraft and ships were frequently infuriated by
being unable to talk reliably to each other.

  Erebus's initial role was to support a British airborne
brigade which landed close to Syracuse. *Roberts* was assigned
a role nearby, also supporting the British landing. The landing
was somewhat chaotic due to the strong winds and errors in
navigation, and instead of calling for fire support at first light
as planned, the Red Berets were not ready to advance until
early afternoon. They were then held up by a strongpoint just
east of the Ponte Grande and, having no artillery of their own,
requested help from the monitor. Twelve terrible 15 inch
rounds, well aimed, were enough to silence the opposition. In
fact one observer was convinced that the very first two rounds
did the trick as the enemy battery stopped firing less than a
minute after *Erebus* opened up. A heavy air attack on shipping
by JU88 bombers and FW190 and ME109 fighters was fought
off, although near misses drenched the decks, and just before
dark another call for fire support on land was received and
once again, at a range of 19,000 yards, an enemy battery was
completely destroyed, this time by only eight rounds. It was
at about this time that a small high speed "Dog Boat" as the
British motor gunboats were called, achieved a remarkable
feat. While operating in support of the two monitors MGB 658
had as her Oerlikon gunner an ex-gamekeeper "Happy" Day.
He brought down two FW190s as they zoomed in towards
him, probably at about 400 mph, with two short and perfectly
timed bursts – just like low, fast, pheasants. There was no
work for the monitor on day two but on day three she was
called on just before dawn to silence the coastal batteries
defending the port of Augusta, just north of Syracuse. The

port could become a useful asset to the invaders as it was a major Italian naval base. Seven separate targets around it were engaged and destroyed close to the point known as San Croce, then fire was shifted to a battery at Melilli a little way inland, *Roberts* and *Erebus* were joined in this bombardment by three heavy cruisers. By nightfall Augusta was open to the Allies.

The next target was a tougher nut to crack, the town of Catania, outside which the advance on land was halted. *Erebus* engaged the airfield at maximum range doing considerable damage, then again in company with cruisers, shelled coastal batteries. Once again there were determined air attacks, but the monitor miraculously remained undamaged. After less than a week's activity *Erebus* had expended all her ammunition and had to return to Malta for more. *Roberts* took over the task of suppressing German forces around Catania and achieved some notably successful shooting. At one point she brought down a tall factory chimney with her first round causing consternation to enemy troops retreating along a nearby road. Arriving back on station off the coast, *Erebus* was welcomed by a savage air raid, during which she was straddled by a stick of bombs which killed six men on deck and wounded twenty-six others, the damage to the ship was light however so repairs were soon effected with the help of *Roberts*'s shipwrights who were nearby and luckily were equipped with welding gear. The next day she fired on a German position which was stubbornly holding out close to Catania. By this time it was clear that Sicily could not be held by the Axis, and all the ships could do was to harass their withdrawal. Unfortunately no one seems to have thought about cutting off the enemy retreat across the Strait of Messina. The Strait was too narrow for large ships to operate and was defended by heavy guns on land, but would have made a perfect hunting ground for motor gunboats and other small craft and for ground attack aircraft. Neither British nor American forces however made any attempt to cover this narrow stretch of water. The retreating Germans were allowed to cross it unmolested in a fleet of large, slow, clumsy barges. The Germans thus successfully landed some five divisions of troops and their equipment on the mainland where they were to put up a stubborn resistance. With better planning by the Allies the heavy guns defending the Strait of Messina could have been destroyed by the monitors and a large proportion of the retreating army either lost at sea or forced to surrender on the Sicilian side. As it was the monitors had to content themselves with a bombardment of the coast road around Taomina. *Roberts* successfully shelled important tunnels and bridges hampering the retreating enemy forces. All three monitors in company were then ordered to Malta for rest and re-armament while the armies prepared for Operation *Baytown* – the attack on the Italian mainland.

On 30 August they were in position to support the Allied landings, but in the event these were only lightly opposed, *Erebus* did engage some targets north of the Straits near Gioia, and successfully shot up road transport going north. As it seemed that there was not much call for their services *Roberts* and *Abercrombie* were withdrawn to Bizerta, leaving *Erebus* in support of the army. On 8 September she supported a landing further up the coast near Pizzo in the Gulf of St Eufemia, there was a strong German contingent in the area and for a time the fighting was severe before the Germans disengaged again and continued northwards. *Erebus* was able to hasten them on their way with twenty-five rounds and was herself a target for coastal artillery and FW190 fighter bombers but she escaped unscathed. Her guns however had now fired almost 400 rounds apiece and were badly worn. She withdrew to Malta once again. In a later chapter we shall see how her sisters fared as the campaign progressed. On 18 September she joined a convoy bound for England and went into Devonport for a refit in readiness for a far more ambitious seaborne invasion – Operation *Neptune* – the naval component of D-Day.

Chapter 8

Erebus and *Roberts* in the Normandy Invasion

E rebus emerged from Devonport laden with a new topmast, a mizzen and air warning radars, as well as enhanced anti-aircraft armament in the form of four twin 20mm Mark 5 quick firing guns for close air defence. She now had no less than five radar sets:

Two type 285 gunnery control for the 4 inch secondary armament. This provided accurate range and bearing information but had poor height finding ability and could not lock onto an incoming target.

Type 79B air warning radar. This was one of the earliest air warning radars designed to pick up incoming aircraft at up to 20 miles range.

Type 272 surface warning radar. This was an advanced centimetric radar capable of picking up small surface targets and providing accurate range and bearings.

Type 276 combined warning/target indication set. This was also a centimetric radar used for directing the main armament, *Erebus* was one of the first ships to be fitted with it.

All this technology and the crews, generators, and stores

to go with it increased her draft so much that the bulges were completely under water, and with only 5 feet of freeboard her decks became extremely wet even in moderate weather. Always difficult to handle she was now a "regular pig" to steer and her best speed was reduced to a little over 11 knots.

Thus modernised and encumbered *Erebus* moved up to the Clyde to join a force of British and American battleships practicing for the forthcoming great event. The Salerno landing (described in a following chapter) had shown the Allied armies what naval bombardment could do in support of an amphibious landing – a most important lesson for officers planning the far greater D-Day landings in Europe. Naval guns could prevent the enemy from concentrating forces in order to stamp out a beachhead, or indeed from moving at all during the crucial early stages of a landing, before land based artillery could be deployed. Unlike aircraft, ships could operate in misty weather and they were particularly effective against tanks, however well they were armoured.

In order to make the most of Allied naval firepower during training for the D-Day operation, particular emphasis was placed on getting good communications established with spotting aircraft (normally Spitfires). The battleships training for shore bombardment alongside the monitors were an elderly bunch, there was *Rodney* (16 inch) laid down in 1922, *Ramillies* (15 inch) (1913), and the USS *Texas* (14 inch) (1911), nevertheless they were all twice as fast as *Erebus* and *Roberts*, and of course they had far heavier protective armour. The squadron was joined by *Roberts* in May 1944, and this venerable force steamed south at the end of the month to take their place among the ships supporting the Allied landings. *Erebus* was then designated to support the US VII Corps landing on Utah Beach (see map 10). This was commanded by Major

General "Lightening Joe" Collins and the naval element, consisting of the battleship *Nevada*, three American heavy cruisers, two British light cruisers and *Erebus*, together with supporting destroyers, came under Rear Admiral Alan Kirk, USN. The foreshore had been heavily attacked during the night from the air. Troops got ashore quite rapidly, and met only sporadic resistance. Unlike at Omaha Beach to their left, almost all their amphibious tanks survived the short "swim" ashore and they quickly established local superiority.

The air attacks had not, however silenced the German heavy guns and *Erebus* was quickly called upon to silence a battery near Quineville on the left flank of the invading party. With the poor luck which often seemed to dog her efforts, the anchor cable was parted by her first bombardment, and it was over an hour before she could resume firing. When she did resume she concentrated on the three 8.3 inch Skoda guns of the St Marcouf Battery nearby, scoring a direct hit on one gun and silencing the battery forever. Later in the day she was called upon to target a radar station inland which seemed to be controlling the fire of other heavy guns. As she opened fire there was a terrible concussion which shook the whole ship. Thinking that there had been a direct hit on the turret, an officer rushed into it to find the occupants reeling about senselessly and a ghastly scene of destruction and chaos, but this was not the doing of the enemy. A shell had burst half way down the barrel of one of the guns, splitting the gun open and wrenching its supports out of line. By some miracle the breech had held and there were no lethal injuries. It was, however, a delicate situation. The damaged barrel might break off and fall clean through the deck, or the charge in the other gun, which had not been fired, might "cook off" and blow that to pieces as well. There was nothing for it but to withdraw from the battle and wait at anchor until a convoy was returning to Portland. A little luck, however awaited the ship on the voyage home. She was asked to evacuate 150 US glider pilots who had completed their dangerous task. The passengers were accommodated in the ship's officer's cabins, which allowed the officers to claim an extremely generous subsistence allowance from the US military, paying off months of mess bills.

As soon as there was dockyard capacity available the damaged barrel was cut away and the ship remained on standby with only one barrel available. An investigation into the cause of the damage concluded that a faulty fuse in the US-made shell she had tried to fire had caused it to explode almost as soon as the cordite propellant was detonated. Two weeks later *Erebus* was under the heavy lift dockyard cranes again and a new barrel and cradle fitted. After a few days testing, the turret was declared fit for service and she steamed back to the foray. By this time (late July 1944) the Allies had consolidated their beachhead but the Germans were fighting back strongly and progress on land was slow. German officers who had been transferred from the Russian front commented that they had never encountered fighting in Russia of anything like the intensity they found in Normandy, where great masses of troops, tanks and artillery were compressed into a relatively small space. Much of the fighting was now several miles inland, out of range of cruisers' fire and most of the battleships had been withdrawn, so *Erebus* and *Roberts*, with their long range guns, were the only ships able to give support. Between 25 July and 14 August, *Erebus* engaged shore batteries and enemy concentrations from a position just off the coast at Courseulles-sur-Mer, equidistant from Caen and Bayeux.

She was attended by a tug to help her keep in position in the tidal stream. So close to the enemy held port of Le Havre, her situation off the coast was dangerous and she was exposed both to night bombing and to attacks by her old adversaries, explosive motor boats, and midget submarines, however she suffered no damage and got off 150 rounds. Often she had to deploy "window" to fox German radar, and smoke against visually aimed shore based artillery.

Roberts meanwhile had been active in support of the British landings on Sword beach, suppressing heavy batteries close to Houlgate in advance of the landing itself. This was made difficult by extensive smokescreens laid both by the defenders and by Allied aircraft attempting to protect the left flank of the Allied landings. She was attacked by torpedo boats emerging from Le Havre whilst she was anchored in her bombarding position, but the torpedoes missed. Luckily, during the initial landings, what German counter fire there was seemed to be concentrated ineffectively on the ships out at sea rather than the landing craft and they did not do much damage. As the troops landed, *Roberts* provided fire support with the assistance of observation officers with the leading troops and enemy coastal artillery fire was effectively smothered. *Roberts* then switched her fire back to Houlgate during the afternoon, managing direct hits on the guns and the ammunition dumps to the delight of the spotting Spitfire pilot. Later that night however a problem arose. The right hand gun burst its jacket hurling bits of metal into the air dangerously close to the ship's bridge. Fire was halted and the ship returned to Portsmouth. After a brief inspection it was decided to return to action with only the left hand gun serviceable because the long range fire of the monitor was desperately needed in support of the British advance on

Villers-Bocage. For the next few days she was kept extremely busy firing on enemy concentrations and armour. By day, spotting was by aircraft and at night "area bombardments" were carried out covering suspected enemy positions. At one point she was joined by the 16 inch battleship *Rodney* for a continuous bombardment of a bridge which Panzers were trying to cross 20 miles inland. This one shoot was sustained for 30 hours. The ship was heeled 3 degrees to achieve maximum range. Together the battleship and monitor effectively neutralised a whole Panzer formation. The British forces were particularly enthusiastic about making use of the heavy guns of the fleet and as a result ammunition supply and barrel wear were constant problems for both the monitors. On 14 June, *Roberts* had to return to Portsmouth to have a new barrel fitted, then resumed her station on the eastern flank, knocking out a succession of enemy artillery positions. During these operations there was constant danger from enemy mines laid at night time by aircraft. Many of these were pressure mines which exploded when they sensed the pressure wave generated by a ship moving close to them, these were almost impossible to sweep so the ship moved as little as possible, doing most of her shooting at anchor.

As June wore on the crucial point of fighting in the British sector came to be the area around Caen, well within range of *Robert*'s guns. The area was infested by German protected concrete strongpoints which 15 inch armour piercing rounds alone could destroy, and destroy them she did. She had an especially satisfactory shoot at a critical road junction which was in theory just beyond her range. Fire was required urgently to prevent an enemy movement and there was no time to heel the ship by flooding a bulge. The gunnery officer came up with the brilliant idea of firing one initial salvo, the recoil of which would heel the ship, then, before she could recover, follow it with another which would of course travel significantly further. The Canadian troops who she was supporting at this point were so impressed with this performance that they sent a large delegation over by DUKW to congratulate the ship.

Churchill decided to visit the battlefield himself and got a good impression of what his early brainchild, the monitor, was now up to as his landing craft passed *Roberts* while she was standing offshore. Just as he passed *Roberts* received an urgent call for fire support from inland and the terrific blast of her 15 inch gun going off so close shook the Prime Minister's little craft almost to pieces and undoubtedly impressed its occupants.

Roberts's last action off Normandy was in support of Operation *Goodwood* the British and Canadian push south west of Caen starting on 18 July. Once again she successfully smashed German artillery and tank concentrations, making an effective counter attack impossible. After this she was replaced on the front line by the repaired *Erebus*. She had fired 692 rounds of 15 inch ammunition and earned the well-deserved trust of the army she had supported. She withdrew to Portsmouth for overhaul and replacement of both barrels of her guns.

As the fighting moved steadily eastwards, Le Havre itself became a prime objective. The port city had been declared a "Festung" by Hitler, a town to be held at all costs, it was heavily defended to seaward by batteries ranging from 3 inch to an enormous 15 inch emplacement at Octeville, just north of the town. This last was not quite complete when the invasion took place and the area had been heavily bombed from the air, but there was a suspicion that at least one of the three heavy guns might be usable. The town had proved an especially tough nut to crack and had been bypassed by the Allied armies who by this time had thrust right through Belgium into Holland. As the British 1 Corps attacked the city on land, *Erebus* was tasked with destroying the batteries and providing heavy gun support. The port was still being used by torpedo boats and midget submarines so her berth offshore, about 12 miles north-west of the port, was dangerous and needed constant watchfulness on behalf of the crew. The first target was a battery of 6.7 inch guns ashore, these were engaged but replied, scoring a hit on the ship's bulge which flooded and caused her to list about 3 degrees. Making smoke she opened the range to examine the damage and it was judged serious enough to return to Portsmouth for a temporary repair. Three days later she was back in action but was soon hit again by the same opponent. This time the shell did not explode and damage was slight so *Erebus* continued her bombardment in spite of the live projectile rolling about inside her bulge. The enemy resisted stubbornly and during the night of 10 August the RAF bombed the front line heavily. The next day *Erebus* was joined by the old battleship *Warspite* in a concentrated strafing of the defenders, spotting aircraft reported excellent shooting with almost thirty per cent direct hits on designated targets. This combination of air strikes and heavy shelling from the sea at last broke the morale of the defenders and when the army launched its final assault on 12 September the garrison surrendered. A special message of thanks was sent to the ships from commander of the troops ashore.

During the Normandy operation, support from warships had been tremendously helpful to the invaders, providing heavy and extremely accurate fire. If he could see the target an observation officer ashore only had to give its co-ordinates to a ship and it could frequently be engaged immediately. Targets invisible to ground troops could often be spotted by the patrolling fighter aircraft. Air strikes by ground attack aircraft were also very effective, especially against vehicles on the move, but communications were often difficult and the pilots had to abort many attacks because they could not make out clearly where the front line was. Heavy high level area bombing of enemy troop positions, by contrast, frequently yielded only disappointing results. Often the target was missed altogether, and even if the bombs did land on enemy forces, it was found that well dug in troops were seldom put out of action. Sometimes indeed the great craters left by the bombs formed an improvised defensive earthwork. It was noticeable that as troops moved further inland, out of the range of naval guns, progress became much slower. Another factor to be considered in respect of bombing from the air was the terrible losses inflicted on civilians, in the case of the battle for Normandy, of course, French. Over 12,500 civilian buildings in Le Havre were destroyed by bombing, 5,000 townspeople were killed and 80,000 rendered homeless. The precision of a naval bombardment stands in sharp contrast to this awful toll. Field-Marshall von Runstedt, perhaps the most intelligent of the German commanders, cited naval bombardment as one of the principal reasons for the success of the Allied invasion of Europe. Once targeted from the sea the heaviest tanks and the most formidable artillery had no option but to hide themselves and hope for the best, and troops came to dread the terrible impact of incoming naval ordnance.

Erebus remained off the coast until 11 September when she returned to Portsmouth for a more permanent repair. In the dockyard the unexploded 6.7 inch shell was found inside the bulge and gingerly removed. When this had been completed she was joined in the Solent by *Roberts* and the two took turns to standby in readiness for further army support operations. In the event, the monitors were not needed until November, when the old ship was to set off for her last operational mission. Ironically this was to be similar to the operation for which monitors were originally designed. It is worth describing this operation in some detail as it resembles in some respects the schemes hatched by Bacon for an armed landing on the Belgian coast in the First World War.

Chapter 9

The Walcheren Landings

The island of Walcheren is an artificial island reclaimed from the sea over many centuries (see map 11). It is essentially a saucer shaped area about 12 miles across and protected from the sea by high artificial sandbanks. The interior consists of fertile agricultural land, at the centre of which is the town of Middelburg. Most of the land and the residential area are below sea level at high tide. To seaward of the protecting sandbanks, the shore consists of soft mud and loose sand. The island is separated from the mainland at its eastern end by an area of mudflats crossed by a road and rail bridge. A canal is cut through the island connecting the West Scheldt to the south to the East Scheldt on the northern side. The vital importance of Walcheren lies in its strategic situation covering the waterway leading to the great port of Antwerp. Antwerp had been captured by the British 11th Armoured Division on 4 September 1944 but was unusable as a seaport because the enemy still held both banks of the Scheldt, and Walcheren itself. Now that British and American troops were pushing eastwards, deep into occupied Europe, it was becoming vital that the port should become operational. None of the French channel ports, which had been heavily sabotaged by the retreating Germans, were in a

condition to handle the large volumes of supplies needed by
the armies and the artificial mulberry harbour at
Arromanches was clogged with traffic and liable to be
destroyed by the winter gales. Transport of war materials
from Normandy to the front line was becoming a logistical
nightmare. In fact the Allied armies were in severe danger of
making the classic military error of advancing too far ahead
of their lines of communication and becoming easy meat for
a determined counter attack. In these circumstances the
Allied High Command decided that the capture of
Walcheren and the surrounding mainland so as to open up
the port facilities of Antwerp was a top priority. During
October, Canadian troops, in a series of tough engagements,
managed to force the Germans out of the area of the south
bank of the Scheldt, opening the small harbour of Breskens,
less than 2 miles from Vlissingen on the southern coast of
Walcheren, for use by landing craft. Together with the
Scottish 52nd Lowland Division they then cleared the enemy
out of South Beveland, to the east of Walcheren, thus effectively isolating the garrison on the island.

The German High Command, and Hitler himself, were
fully aware of the vital part which Walcheren could play in
holding up the Allied advance. The island was fortified by
eight heavy gun batteries, and these themselves were
protected by flak guns which could be used against both
aircraft and ground troops and vehicles. The heavy artillery
pieces covered every possible landing area, sweeping the
mudflats and sand dunes with enfilading fire. They were
installed in fortified casements with walls 7 feet thick, proof
against anything less than 15 inch artillery. The casement
mounted guns commanded the Scheldt, which was also
sown with moored contact mines, magnetic mines and

controlled ground mines, making any approach to the beaches extremely risky. Massive anti-tank barriers, reinforced by land mines and explosive booby traps, divided the south part of the island, considered the most vulnerable, from the centre and north. The whole island was declared a "Festung", to be defended at all costs. Troops leaving their posts were to be shot by their officers as was anyone seeking to leave the island without orders. There were however some inherent weaknesses in the German position.

The most important of these was the quality of the defending troops. During the early stages of the Second World War, British soldiers had been consistently outfought by the Germans, who had shown toughness, skill and determination which their opponents could not match. By 1944 however the British army had changed dramatically from top to bottom. Battle hardened generals had under their command well trained and equipped troops with an impressive will to succeed in whatever task was set them. The British officers and soldiers designated to attack Walcheren were supplemented by Dutch, Belgian and Norwegian fighters who had escaped their homelands and volunteered to serve with the commandoes. These patriots were to prove doughty fighters. By contrast the German garrison troops defending Walcheren were a poor bunch, and badly led. Many of the soldiers were semi-invalids and their commander Lieutenant General Daser was himself old and ill. The coastal guns, however, which were the mainstay of the defence, were manned by German naval personnel who were fit, determined, and extremely skilful. Liaison between the naval artillerymen and the army however was not good and this was to prove a critical weakness. Furthermore the once formidable Luftwaffe was so short of fuel and of trained pilots that it could offer little support. Its efforts were concentrated on the defence of the Reich against Allied bombers, and on occasional night time mine laying operations. On their part the British had developed excellent techniques for inter service co-operation in carrying out amphibious operations. The incomparable Admiral Ramsay, who had planned the Sicily and the Normandy landings, was the brains behind the scheme for assaulting Walcheren and was able to gain the commitment of British and Canadian air, land and sea forces to the successful execution of this complex and dangerous mission.

The naval bombardment contingent of the attacking force was commanded by Captain Anthony Pugsley whose previous appointments had mainly been in destroyers, his force consisted of minesweepers, a handful of destroyers, motor gunboats and three heavy gunships, the old battleship *Warspite, Roberts* and *Erebus*. Cruisers were not used because their guns were not sufficiently powerful to put the coastal batteries out of action and their deep draft made it impossible for them to get close inshore. *Warspite* had only two of her turrets working and the guns of those were close to the end of their lives. The main naval bombardment effort would therefore have to be put in by the monitors. Spotting was to be provided by Spitfires and by forward observation teams ashore. A glance at the map will show that the south part of the island was well within range of land based artillery ashore near Breskins, the British and Canadian armies had a formidable battery there including the superb 5.5 inch guns of the medium artillery units, and a handful of heavier weapons. These would be sufficient to at least keep the enemy heads down in the south of the island, but to the west and north German positions were out of effective range of shore based artillery and would be the main focus of the naval bombardment effort. A vitally important role in the fighting would be played by Spitfire and Typhoon ground attack aircraft based in France.

As well as their artillery, the attacking soldiers and marines had a useful selection of vehicles, the most important of which were Buffalo amphibious tracked vehicles carrying up to thirty troops and able to make 7 mph in the water and 25 mph on land. Many of them were modified by fitting a turret with a quick firing gun, giving them the appearance of a small tank. There were also armoured bull-dozers, AVREs (Armoured Vehicle Royal Engineers) fitted with demolition guns, mine clearing flails or ditch crossing equipment, and a small number of Sherman and Churchill tanks. Unfortunately for the attackers no proper survey of the beaches was possible before the attack as the shore was too heavily guarded to permit a reconnaissance party to land. As a result the unexpected soft mud and sand trapped many of the tracked vehicles as soon as they got to shore, so that well over half of them had to be abandoned.

The attack on the island began with concentrated bombing by RAF Lancasters of what were considered to be the weak points of the dykes around the island. They attacked in daylight, guided in by pathfinding Mosquitoes. To the surprise of some of those involved this was successful and four large breaches were made during the early part of October, allowing the sea to come in, flooding most of the farm land and the lower lying parts of the towns. This also had the effect of isolating the German positions, making it very difficult for them to support each other. In the cold autumn weather and storms, Walcheren, flooded and cut off as it was, must have been an extremely uncomfortable billet for the German occupation forces. The heavy gun batteries, however, situated on dry ground on top of the surrounding dykes and sand dunes were largely unaffected.

On 1 November the main attack began. Well before first light commandos landed at the docks at Vlissingen, catching the defenders off guard and capturing the town, apart from a few strong points, quite rapidly. A second landing in daylight at Westkapelle was more problematic. Buffaloes and landing craft came under effective fire from on land and got hopelessly stuck in mud and soft sand on the beaches. Most of the commandos eventually got ashore with only their small arms, floundering through the mud, and these managed to establish a sustainable beachhead. Their role of getting to the batteries along the sand dunes and knocking them out without the support of most of their armoured vehicles was going to be extremely challenging, as they had to advance on a narrow front along the dunes into the face of defending fire from small arms, machine guns, flack guns and mortars. The dunes themselves were strewn with obstacles and mines. Covering fire from the heavy guns of British ships at sea would be critical.

The bombardment squadron was 11 miles off shore so as to keep clear of sandbanks and minefields. Unfortunately when the landing at Westkapple took place the spotting aircraft had been grounded by fog at Manston and so the great guns had to be sighted visually. *Warspite* opened up at 8.15 AM targeting the heavy battery at Domburg while *Roberts* successfully knocked out the enemy radar station nearby. *Erebus* had been designated the coastal battery W15 at Westkapelle but her turret training gear had broken down and her target had to be assigned to *Roberts* until the gear was repaired by 9.30. Both ships then concentrated on W15 until the commandos were too close to allow firing to continue. *Roberts* made excellent shooting hitting the target directly, killing thirty of the gunners, and so stunning the rest that they were temporarily out of action. This one shoot probably was pivotal for the whole Westkapelle landing. It would have been impossible to sustain the beachhead with W15 in action. Both ships then switched to W13 battery, they were still firing visually, without spotters, because the observation officer on land had unfortunately been killed almost as soon as he landed.

As the morning wore on the fog lifted and air spotting became available, all three ships concentrating on W13, W15, which had somehow managed to get back into action and Domburg which was also now in action again in spite of *Warspite*'s bombardment. All of these were severely damaged then captured by the end of the day after ferocious fighting, in every case the gunners had been stunned by the close impact of heavy shells and had also suffered from devastating attacks by rocket firing Typhoon aircraft. As darkness fell the heavy ships withdrew to avoid possible torpedo boat attack, *Warspite* returning to England, her guns finally worn out. She was perhaps the most famous and successful British battleship of the war, and this was to be her last offensive operation.

Next morning the monitors were back in action again, first knocking out a flak battery which had been troubling the spotting aircraft, then hammering the W11 battery which had repaired some of the damage caused the previous day and was seriously hampering Allied operations ashore. *Erebus* made some particularly good shooting this day although she still had problems with her turret working gear so that men were operating most of the time in a chamber flooded a foot deep in water. Out of ninety-nine rounds fired, twenty-seven were direct hits on the battery and most of the rest were close to the target; the command post and range finder were destroyed by a direct hit and two shells struck the actual gun casements themselves. This multiple battery, equipped with field guns, flack guns and heavy artillery was a particularly tough nut for the commandos ashore to tackle as it was protected by strong infantry positions equipped with machine guns and mortars, and an anti-tank wall consisting of concrete "dragon's teeth" festooned with explosive devices. It did not finally fall until early the next day and when it did the attackers found the eerie spectacle gun crews sitting round their weapons seemingly unhurt but actually killed by the effect of the blast of the 15 inch shells from the sea.

This was the last day of action for the monitors, the coastal batteries had fallen and the soldiers and marines ashore had only to complete the job of mopping up pockets of resistance. The 52nd Lowland Division (incidentally this was designated as a "Mountain Division" with appropriate special equipment. It was ironic that it conducted its first operation on a battlefield below sea level), managed to flounder across the mud separating the island from South Beveland and opened a new front on the east side of Walcheren. Middleburg fell to a small patrol of Norwegians approaching from Westkapelle. In an amusing incident the Norwegian lieutenant leading the patrol took the surrender of General Daser the festung's commanding officer. Aware that the general would not surrender to a lowly lieutenant, the resourceful Norwegian borrowed pips and other badges of rank from all the officers with him and presented himself to the Daser in the assumed guise of a "staff colonel" – a rank which has never existed. By 8 November, after exactly a week of fighting, all organised resistance ceased. By 26th the channel up the Scheldt was open, the minefields cleared by an extremely efficient naval sweeping operation. It was to be a crucial event in the war, without Antwerp and the supplies which came flooding in through its port, the Allies might well have been unable to withstand the fearsome Ardennes Offensive which was to come that winter.

Both monitors returned to home waters for the remainder of the war, standing in readiness to support the Allied advance into Germany but they were not called for. *Roberts* was then dispatched to the Far East, but the end of the war came before she reached the Indian Ocean. She returned to Devonport where she was employed in various training and accommodation roles until being broken up in the 1960s. *Erebus* had a brief post war career as a turret drill ship at Chatham, departing to the breaker's yard in 1946.

The Walcheren episode provides not only a good example of monitors being used in their proper role, but also gives a clue as to the outcomes which might have been expected from Bacon's proposed raids on the Belgian coast in the First World War and indeed the landings on the north German coast which Churchill and Fisher had advocated and for which monitors had been originally conceived. Walcheren was in almost every respect an easier task than any of these. The island was totally isolated. By the time the attack took place, the enemy could not re-supply or reinforce it. Only 2 miles to the south the port of Breskens was in Allied hands, artillery from there could support beachheads, and in the sheltered waters of the Scheldt, small craft could operate safely in most weather conditions. The attackers had at their disposal a range of excellent amphibious vehicles unimagined in the First World War. Most important of all the Allies had almost complete air superiority and could call down the massive offensive power of the Typhoons and Spitfires on pockets of resistance and of the Lancasters to provide heavy bombing when required. Even with all these advantages the Allies were involved in some tough fighting and the outcome at times looked as if it was in balance. If the defending infantry had fought with the courage and skill which was typical of German combat troops, the invaders might well have been thrown back into the sea. In the light of these facts it is difficult to see much prospect for success for Bacon's Great Landing on an exposed beach which the enemy could readily reinforce, swept by fire from the batteries, and using only the most primitive and unreliable armoured vehicles.

Chapter 10

The Final Phase in the Mediterranean

We must now return to 1941 and the beginning of the story of *Roberts* and of her sister ship *Abercrombie*. The Royal Navy hoped that *Roberts*, which became operational in October of that year, would emulate the fine performance achieved by *Terror* in the early part of the north African campaign. In company with *Erebus* she made her stately way round the Cape of Good Hope, stopping in Simonstown on 11 January 1942, and then at Durban for boiler repairs, *Erebus* then being diverted to Trincomalee, as we have seen. By the time *Roberts* reached Suez, Rommel had pushed the British Army back almost to Alexandria and there was not much the monitors could do in the Mediterranean so *Roberts* was ordered to act as anti-aircraft guard ship stationed about 3 miles off Suez. She had, of course been fitted with early warning and gun control radar so was much better suited for the task than the unfortunate *Terror* had been. At Suez however the task proved to be a hot and boring one, as very few air raids took place. By July the situation on the ground had changed and the Allies were planning their landings in North Africa. *Roberts* was dispatched to Gibraltar, again via the Cape, to provide heavy gun support. She was extremely foul after spending so long at anchor off Suez, and had to pause on the way to scrape her bottom, and did not reach her destination until November. She was just in time to sail in support of the Allied landings at Algiers.

The Italian fleet was still, at least in theory, operational, and there was a considerable risk that it might try to interfere with the landings so all the available heavy ships were required to protect the invasion force, leaving *Roberts* as the only powerful bombardment ship giving close support to the invasion. In the event she was not needed, the Vichy forces in Algeria made little effort to repel the invaders, depriving the monitor of the chance to make use of her main armament. The Luftwaffe however was a different matter. Junkers 87 and 88 aircraft mounted savage attacks on ships offshore so *Roberts* was designated to act as radar picket again and this time she had plenty for her anti-aircraft guns to do. Two days later she moved to carry out a similar role at Bougie, a short distance further east. Here there was no fighter protection for the Allied convoys as it had been impossible to land supplies for the land based aircraft designated to cover the landings, and the only available aircraft carrier had been damaged. Once again *Roberts* put up a spirited defence, bringing down at least one aircraft. Nevertheless two troopships were sunk and late in the evening the Germans, realising that *Roberts* was a key to the air defences, made a concentrated attack on her. One Ju88 came in from the bow and two from the stern scoring two direct hits and one near miss. In spite of her 4 inch main deck armour the damage was severe and the casualty list long. One bomb hit the bulge on the port side level with the funnel holing it and allowing the inner compartments to flood. The blast also started a fire on the main deck which was quickly brought under control. The second 500lb missile hit the ship just aft of the funnel and smashed down as far as the armoured main deck starting fires on its way and destroying the engine room ventilation system. This was serious as without ventilation the engine room was untenable. The total "butcher's bill" was seventeen dead and thirty-five wounded. The fight had to go on however and, disabled as she was, *Roberts* continued to provide anti-aircraft cover, supplementing her gun crews with men from sunken ships nearby. The radars were repaired and a temporary ventilation system rigged up using parts from mess deck fans, so she became mobile again and fought on, providing radar early warning and fire support to the landing force until Spitfires from Djidelli at last became operational and drove off the attackers. The last serious attack she suffered was from two torpedo bombers which came in straight and low, launching their weapons accurately at their target. Luckily for the wounded ship the enemy had not allowed for her shallow draft and the torpedoes passed harmlessly beneath her (torpedoes fired by aircraft were normally set to run about 20 feet deep when used against large ships. *Roberts* only drew 14 feet). In a quiet period some flooded compartments were pumped out and holes sealed with concrete. As the enemy air threat diminished however it became clear that major repairs to her hull were essential, and she sailed for Gibraltar and then on home to Liverpool for major repairs. She had fought well in a difficult role and her stout defensive armour had proved very effective.

Abercrombie was the last monitor to be built, being completed, after many delays, in May 1943. She was fully equipped with anti-aircraft radar and radar direction for her main armament and thus was heavier at 9,150 tons (deep) and drew more water (14 foot 5 in) than any previous monitor. She joined up with the freshly repaired *Roberts* and the two sailed for the Mediterranean in May 1943. During the voyage *Roberts* had a problem due to losing a turbine blade in one turbo generators. This was potentially serious because no spares were available and if her other generator failed she would be out of action.

On their arrival *Roberts* was ordered to work with *Erebus* to support the British landings on Sicily, described in a previous chapter, while *Abercrombie* embarked a US liaison officer and a signals team to work with the American landings further west. Nicknamed "Little Dumbo" by the Americans she was not short of work to do. She arrived on station off the beaches on 10 July, her first target was troop concentrations around Comiso airfield, which were heavily bombarded until a more serious threat to the US landings, in the form of a strong armoured counter attack, developed. She opened fire at a range of 30,000 yards and quickly destroyed the enemy headquarters while cruisers and destroyers shot up targets closer to the shore. She then switched to an enemy gun battery, knocking out five field guns with five rounds, then delighted troops on the shore by obtaining a direct hit on a tank leading a charge down a hillside towards them. This was excellent work, made more difficult as the spotting aircraft allocated, US seaplanes, could not operate because the Allies did not have air superiority over western Sicily at this point. Spotting thus had to be carried out by observers on the ground who themselves had difficulty in seeing what was going on and identifying targets. As the invaders consolidated their beachhead and moved inland *Abercrombie* had less to do for the next few days until the enemy brought into play heavy guns, including a railway mounted battery, close to Agrigento. By now air superiority had been established, allowing the spotting seaplanes to be deployed. "Little Dumbo" and the cruisers together quickly dealt with this threat, destroying the guns in short order. After a week's good work she returned to Malta for ammunition.

Returning to the foray she found that the enemy had retreated further inland and she switched her role to anti-aircraft picket for a while, before returning again to Malta, meeting up with *Erebus* and *Roberts,* to prepare for the invasion of the Italian mainland.

Erebus supported the initial landings on the toe of Italy before returning, her guns worn out, to the UK. *Roberts* and *Abercrombie* were allocated to support the Allied landings behind the enemy front lines, at Salerno. They sailed for Bizerta, *Roberts* to join the British landing force which was to form the northern wing of the assault, "Little Dumbo" again working with the Americans to the south. On 9 September the force landed facing well organised German opposition ashore (Italy had now withdrawn from the war). *Abercrombie* was soon in action, firing at targets well inland while at the same time beating off determined attacks from enemy aircraft. She successfully engaged a tank concentration, again scoring direct hits in spite of misty weather making air observation difficult. The Germans had been forewarned of a possible landing at Salerno and had mined the area heavily so that Royal Navy minesweepers were kept busy clearing a path for the bombarding ships. Unfortunately there had not been time to buoy the cleared areas properly and *Abercrombie* drifted into an unswept zone. Just after 5.00 PM she struck a large moored contact mine, estimated to contain 500lbs of explosive. This tore open her protective bulge and left her with a 10 degree list to starboard. To correct this, the port bulge was flooded, causing her to float very deep in the water. Damage to the main parts on the ship had been slight, and thanks to her bulges she could still steam and manoeuvre. There was only one serious casualty. The ship had no welding gear aboard (*Roberts* had purchased her welding equipment privately in South Africa) but as usual the US Navy was well equipped with support services and the US tug *Moreno* came alongside and helped to make temporary repairs. *Abercrombie* was then able to depart for Palermo under her own steam. The most serious damage was to her vital fire director control system which made it impossible for her to make use of her main armament. US soldiers ashore must have been sad to see that they would no longer have the support of "Little Dumbo's" killer punch. After temporary repairs in Palermo she went to the Italian dockyard at Taranto, now in Allied hands, where she was fully repaired. From there she was sent to Malta where she set about re-training her crew for further action but luck was not on her side. On 24 August 1944 she struck two more mines, close to the island, these had probably been laid by German aircraft. She was extensively damaged and had to stagger into Grand Harbour for repairs. She never fought again.

Roberts meanwhile had been at work further north successfully engaging two targets east of Salerno itself, then shooting up the road to Naples to the north. It was difficult to get good radio communications with observation officers on land in the hilly country, making effective shooting a problem. The ship had some difficulties of her own, the gun director gear failing at one point, and a misfire in one of her guns (later attributed to ammunition salvaged from a sunken ship) putting it out of action. She continued nevertheless to fire using the one undamaged gun on rail junctions and communications. A strong German armoured counter attack on 12 September sliced through the gap between the British and American forces on land and threatened to force them to withdraw, until it was checked by naval gunfire on 14th, although *Roberts* did not participate in this, she did successfully bring down at least one enemy aircraft and shot up the enemy headquarters in Cava, making a successful night time shoot accurately at long range. This was achieved by laying a buoy in a carefully surveyed position in the daytime and calibrating the guns on the target, then returning to the buoy at night, when the Germans were not expecting artillery fire, and firing "blind". On another occasion she got very close inshore and managed to protect some beached landing craft by putting down a heavy smoke screen.

Roberts was having a particularly busy war. She withdrew from the Italian front and had a major refit in Egypt before returning to the UK to join in the biggest amphibious operation of the war – the D-Day landing. This has been described in previous chapters.

Chapter 11

Conclusion

From the start monitors were odd ships, designed in a rush, using engines and guns scavenged from other vessels. They had been specifically intended to form part of a special "shallow draft fleet" designed to operate off the north German coast, as part of an operation which was wisely cancelled at an early stage of the First World War. Nevertheless in both wars they were heavily used and gave sterling service. They were not war changing ships, but for a very limited investment they provided excellent value. There can be no doubt that in both wars naval bombardment played a key role in achieving success. The support of the left flank of the Allied armies in 1914, the advances in North Africa in 1940, the invasion of Sicily, the D-Day landings and the Walcheren landings being prime examples. Heavy gun support could of course be achieved in other ways. In the Pacific war the Americans used battleships extensively in this role. They did an excellent job, but because of their deep draft they had to stand a long way offshore, and several of them were severely damaged by shore based artillery, mines or aircraft, putting an extremely expensive ship and its huge compliment out of action for a considerable time. Monitors would have been a cheaper way of doing the job. In the vastness of the Pacific the slow speed of the British designs would of course have been a severe problem. Nevertheless a radically re-designed ship on the monitor principle, with big guns, shallow draft, good underwater protection, but reasonable speed and handiness, would not have been difficult to design in the 1940s. Such a warship could have become a very useful class of vessel, especially during the island hopping campaign in which US forces were involved. It could have been built and manned for a fraction of the cost of a battleship and could have been speedily constructed in commercial, as opposed to naval, shipbuilding yards.

To a large extent the role occupied by monitors was increasingly assumed by ground attack aircraft during the course of World War Two and one might expect that this would have progressed further in any subsequent conflict, eliminating the need for naval shore bombardment altogether, but recent history presents a slightly different picture. In the Falklands campaign of 1982 the British used destroyers and frigates to bring down pinpoint accurate fire on enemy gun positions hidden among civilian houses around Port Stanley. These were "spotted" by observers on the ground and their impressive precision was achieved by using satellite positioning and accurate mapping – really a refinement of the techniques used by Bacon's monitors in the First World War. Air strikes could not, at the time, have achieved the same precision.

In the late 1970s the US Navy even took four Second World War *Iowa* class 16 inch fast battleships out of mothballs and re-activated them in order to protect their aircraft carriers and to bombard enemy shore positions in the Middle East. The refurbishment took a minimum of two years per ship and was vastly expensive. There was no 16 inch ammunition available which was not long past its "use by" date and practically no one was left in the armed forces who knew how to operate the guns or their control system, nevertheless a crew of 1,600 officers and men had to be found and trained for each ship. Eventually three of them did reach the combat zones and in 1982 *Iowa* opened fire on artillery positions in Lebanon. The bombardment was ineffective, largely because the 40-year-old propellant being used was unreliable resulting in very poor range accuracy. In 1991, during the First Gulf War, *Wisconsin* and *Missouri* fired cruise missiles effectively at targets in Iraq 700-800 miles away, an amazing demonstration of the long reach of sea power, but these missiles could have equally well been launched by a small ship such as a destroyer. In the event the battleships were never called upon to protect aircraft carriers, so reverted to what was more or less a "monitor" role. In fact they needed protection themselves from Iraqi missiles. *Missouri,* for example, would have been sunk or badly damaged in the Persian Gulf by a Chinese made Silkworm missile, if a British destroyer had not been on hand to shoot it down using a Sea Dart interceptor missile. Altogether the use of battleships at this time was an extremely costly error. If big guns were really needed it would have been far cheaper to do exactly what Fisher did in 1914 and salvage the guns from obsolete ships, installing them instead on a cheap, simple, newly built, hull. The resulting new "monitor" could have been fitted to carry a complement of offensive and defensive missiles as well as its guns and could have been a very useful bombardment vessel, much more economical to build, operate and man, than the old battlewagons.

Technology has moved on since the Gulf Wars but not altogether in a way which reduces the role of naval bombardment.

The role of great long range guns has since then been still further eroded by missiles with various sorts of guidance system, and by unmanned aircraft. Also cruise missiles fired from submarines have been developed to become an extremely effective means of bombardment from the sea. Maybe, however, one day in the distant future, great guns may emerge again in a new form. Electro-magnetic guns may, in a future combat, propel aimed projectiles at extremely high velocities accurately at targets far inland, from a ship or a submersible equipped with the necessary generators and electrical storage systems. Such a weapon offers the possibility of being accurately aimed from the ship and of travelling so fast as to be impossible to intercept. It would have the additional advantages of being entirely independent, once fired, of any guidance system with which an enemy could interfere by using electronic counter measures, of having no infra-red radiation for a defensive missile to track, and of being too small, fast and low flying to be an easy radar target.

All this of course is mere speculation. No one, on the other hand, can deny the steadfastness, the skill, the courage, or the devotion of the brave men of all ranks who served in the monitors in both world wars. Exposed to risks considered unacceptable for other types of ship, and used in roles such as anti-aircraft picket for which they were never intended and were inherently unsuitable, they had more of their fair share of difficulties with mechanical reliability and the elements as well as with the enemy. Crews were often elderly and sometimes they and their ancient vessels were figures of fun (*Erebus* was known as *Cerebros* – the home of old salts), but they set a fine example of grit and determination. They brought their extraordinary ships into action in difficult and frequently frustrating circumstances, suffering frequent breakdowns and accidents due to the ancient and unreliable guns and turrets, the inadequate engines and the poor design of the ships themselves. As a result of their efforts the monitor fleet provided Britain with excellent value for money and made a contribution out of all proportion to its cost in both world wars.

Appendix

List of British Monitors 1914 - 1945

Name		In Service	Tonnage
Ex Brazilian Gunboats			
Mersey		1914	1,520
Severn		1914	1,520
Humber		1914	1,520
Ex Norwegian			
Gorgon		1918	5,740
Glatton		1918	5,740
14 inch			
Abercrombie		1915	6,150
Havelock		1915	6,150
Raglan		1915	6,150
Roberts		1915	6,150
12 inch			
Clive		1915	5,900
Rupert		1915	5,900
Moore		1915	5,900
Crauford		1915	5,900
Eugene		1915	5,900
Peterborough		1915	5,900
Picton		1915	5,900
Wolfe		1915	5,900
15 inch first batch			
Ney (D)		1915	6,670
Soult (D)		1915	6,670
15 inch second batch			
Erebus		1916	8,400
Terror		1916	8,400
15 inch final batch			
Roberts	(ST)	1941	9,150
Abercrombie	bie (ST)	1943	9,717
Small Monitors			
M15-28		1915	650
M29-M33		1915	580

Note: Armament of some of these ships was changed to multipule 6 or 4 inch during the war
 (M18-20,M23,M25-M28 Semi Diesel, M24 Paraffin)

(D) = Diesel
(ST) = Steam Turbine
All other ships steam piston engines triple or quadripule expansion/

	Beam	Engines	Speed	Main Armament		Deployed
	(ft)	HP	Kts.			
ins	49	1,450	9.5	2x6 inch & 2x4.7 inch		Belgium, E.Africa, Med
ins	49	1,450	9.5	2x6 inch & 2x4.7 inch		Belgium, E.Africa, Med
ins	49	1,450	9.5	3x6 inch & 2x4.7 inch		Belgium, Med
ins	74	4,000	13	2x9.2 inch & 4x6 inch		
ins	74	4,000	13	2x9.2 inch & 4x6 inch		
ns	90	2,000	7	2x14 inch	Med	
ns	90	2,000	7.3	2x14 inch	Med	
ns	90	2,310	7.6	2x14 inch	Med	
ns	90	1,800	5.7	2x14 inch	Med	
ins	87	2,310	8	2x12 inch	Belgium	
				1X18 inch added		
ins	87	1,600	7	2x12 inch	Belgium	
ins	87	2,500	7.7	2x12 inch	Belgium	
ins	87	2,310	7.4	2x12 inch	Belgium	
ins	87	2,310	8.2	2x12 inch	Belgium	
				1X18 inch added		
ins	87	2,310	7.7	2x12 inch	Med & Adriatic	riatic
ins	87	2,310	7.4	2x12 inch	Med & Adriatic	riatic
ins	87	2,500	8	2x12 inch	Belgium	
				1X18 inch added		
ins	90	1,500	6.3	2x15 inch	Belgium & The Downes	
				Multipule 6 inch later		
ins	90	1,500	6.6	2x15 inch	Belgium	
ins	88	6,000	14	2x15 inch	Belgium Ceylon Med Normandy Walcheren	
ins	88	6,000	13	2x15 inch	Belgium Med	
ins	90	4,800	13	2x15 inch	Med Normandy Walcheren	
ins	90	4,800	12	2x15 inch	Med	
s	31	560-800	11-11.5	1x9.2 inch	various	
ns	31	400	10	2x6 inch	various	

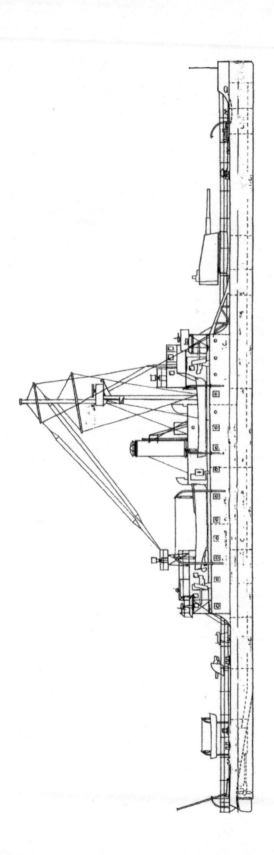

1 Severn

When she was launched *Severn* had the twin 6 inch turret shown here, it was replaced by two single turrets when the first set of guns were worn out after the Belgian Coast operation. Note the very low profile of the hull and the propellers mounted in a tunnel so as to reduce draft.

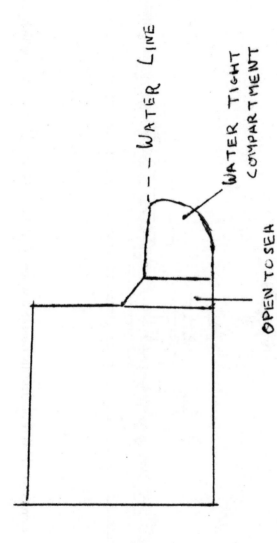

2 Section of Monitor Hull

The bulges protruded well outside the hulls making boat handling extremely difficult. They did afford good protection from underwater weapons and made the ships very stable but slow.

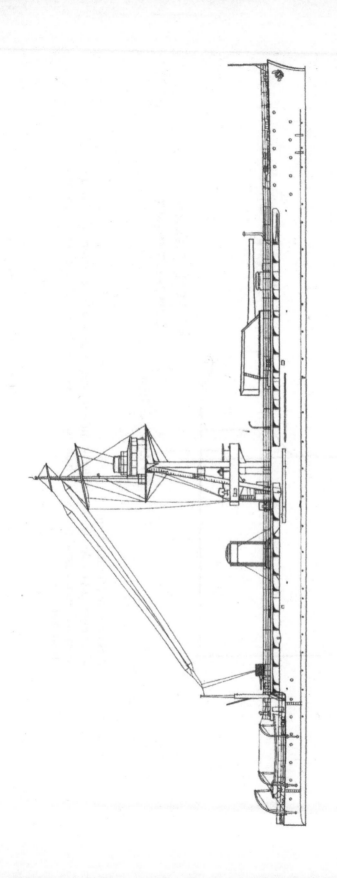

3 A 14 inch Monitor
These ships had U.S. made turrets which were electrically operated where as all Royal Navy experience was with hydraulic operation.

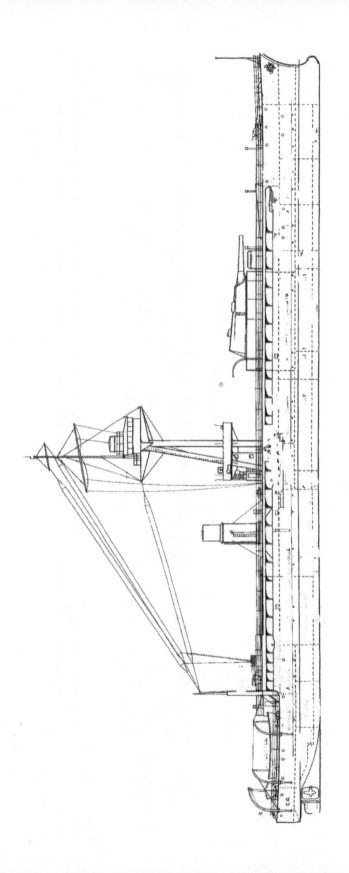

4 A 12 inch Monitor.
These ships proved to have insufficient range to operate against German batteries on the Belgian coast but did good work in net defence and as guard-ships.

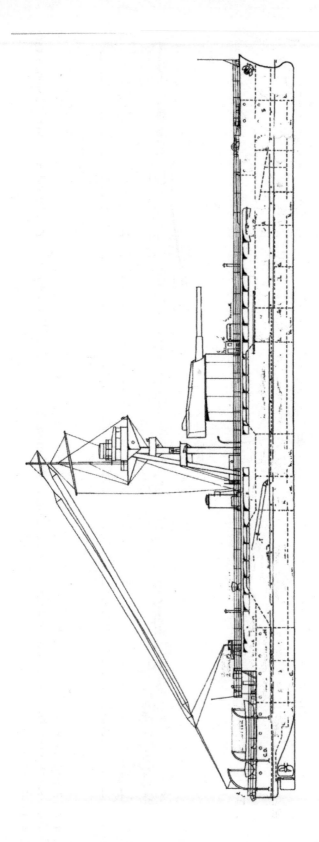

5 Ney

Ney was the least satisfactory of all the monitors as she was so unreliable and slow. The 15 inch turret had to be mounted on top of a column because of the height of the diesel engine beneath it. Her sister ship *Soult* did some good service. Note the short funnel required by the diesel engine.

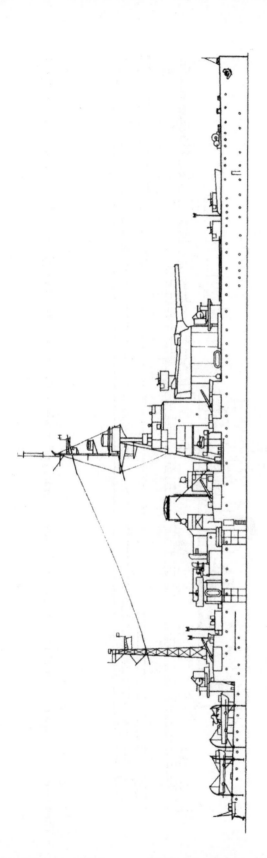

6   Erebus in 1944

Compare the line drawing to photograph no. 6 showing *Erebus* before radar and extra anti-aircraft guns were added. All the extra "clutter" aft made her even more difficult to steer than when she was new. Bacon suggested that she should be fitted with a rudder at the bow so that she could back away from the Belgian coast whilst still using her main armament, but this was never fitted. Note that she has a proper bridge instead of the conning tower fitted to earlier monitors. In a following wind the smoke from the funnel would envelop the bridge to the great annoyance of the watchkeepers.

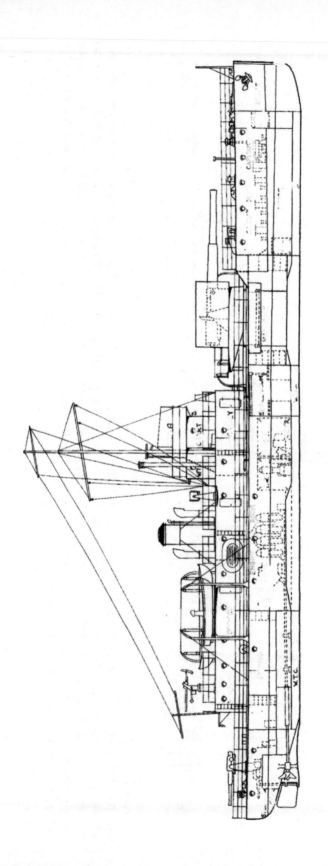

7 A 9.2 inch Small Monitor
These were most useful little ships, cheap to build and operate and moderately sea worthy. They gave excellent service in many theatres.

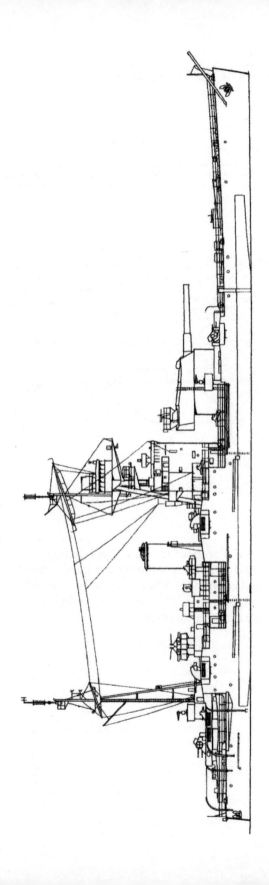

8 Abercrombie

Abercrombie was the last monitor to be built, she spent most of her active life supporting American troops who nicknamed her "Little Dumbo". Note that her bulge now protrudes above the water line which made boat handling much easier. She was fitted with the most up to date radar and fire control equipment as can be seen from the drawing.

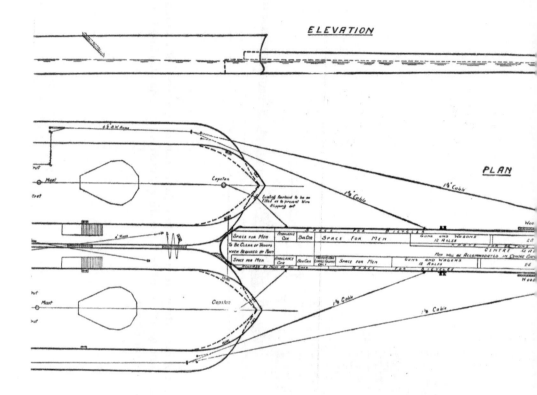

10 Diagram of Monitors and Pontoons for the Great Landing
Two 12 inch monitors would push each of the three pontoons fully
loaded with men, tanks and equipment. The raft in the bows would
run onto the beach against the sea wall to allow men and tanks to
get ashore, covered by fire from the monitors.

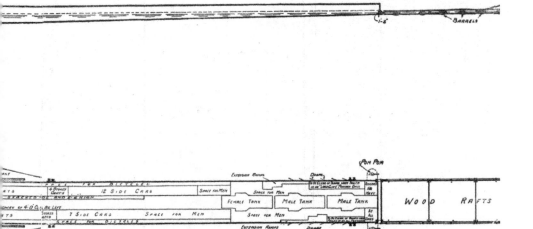

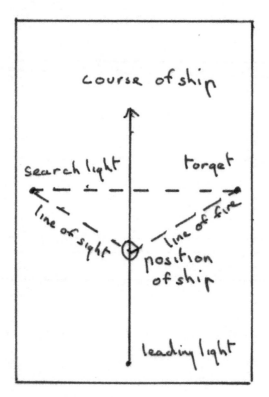

9 System for Night Firing
A ship steaming on a known course at a known range from the target would train its director on a searchlight in a position roughly opposite to the target and fire in the reverse direction to that indicated by the director.

Index